Barns of Aitkin County, Minnesota

Published by
Aitkin County Historical Society

Acknowledgements

The decision to produce a photographic history of barns in Aitkin County, Minnesota was finalized in 2011. Every effort was made to publicize the project and accept information, photos, and stories from those who were interested. If there were some exclusions, it was due to human error or the fact that material was not submitted. Some stories were condensed or re-arranged to avoid duplication or word limitations.

Many hours have been spent producing this book. We would like to thank the following people who helped produce this book: James Ratz, Aitkin County Attorney and Henry Brucker, Attorney; Greg and Laura Thornbloom, photography, design, and layout; Joann Oaks, photography; Hannah Nelson, photography; McGrath Historical Society, Carol Bailey and Darlene Maciej; Julie Hansen, proofreading; Milagros Blakesley-Wicklund, consulting; volunteers of the Aitkin County Historical Society; Aitkin County Land Department; Aitkin Independent Age; and those in the public sector contributed greatly by sharing stories and allowing their barns to be photographed.

The following businesses contributed to the publishing of this book: Mille Lacs Electric Cooperative; Mille Lacs Band of Ojibwe; Memorial from the Kaplan Foundation in the name of KC (Kap) and Hazel Kaplan; American Legion Post #86; Odd Fellow Lodge No. 164; and Aitkin Riverboat Lions.

Greg Leach, Administrator
Aitkin County Historical Society
and Depot Museum

Copyright ©Aitkin County Historical Society, 2013
Copies of this publication may be ordered from the
Aitkin County Historical Society
P.O. Box 215
Aitkin, Minnesota 56431

Photo Credits

Cover: **Greg Thornbloom**

Title Page: Color photo – **Greg Thornbloom,** Black and white photo submitted by **Kerry Hopperstad**

Table of Contents Map: **Milagros Blakesley-Wicklund**

Introduction photos: **Greg Thornbloom**

Carol Bailey: Page 69 (9)

Hannah Nelson: Page 32 (9), page 33 (2, 5, 9), page 34 (1), page 88 (5), page 103 (3)

Joann Oaks: Page 11 (8), page 16 (1,6,7), page 19, (8,9), page 25 (4), page 30 (3), page 31 (3), page 34 (8), page 43 (1,2), page 61 (2), page 62 (3), page 72 (4), page 79 (3), page 88 (8), page 89 (4), page 99 (6,7), page 100 (1,7), page 104 (3), 118 (1)

All other photos: **Greg and Laura Thornbloom** unless noted

**Published by the
Aitkin County Historical Society
Depot Museum
Aitkin, Minnesota**
First Edition: 2013

All rights reserved. No part of this book may be used or reproduced in any manner whatsoever without written permission in writing from the publisher.

ISBN: 978-1-62890-296-9

Printed in the United States of America
by Bang Printing
Brainerd, Minnesota

Table of Contents

4
A Barn is a Barn is a Barn – Not!

5
Introduction

6
Photo Directions Index

10
Aitkin County Map

11
Photographs of Barns

108
Aitkin County Centennial and Sesquicentennial Farms

109
Styles, conditions, foundations, winter, outbuildings, interiors and exteriors, equipment, silos

117
The Barns are Standing

153
The Barns are Gone

180
McGrath Historical Society

A Barn is a Barn is a Barn – Not!
By Donohue Sarff – June 2012

A famous person once said: "A rose, is a rose, is a rose." Perhaps a not-so-famous person said: "A barn is a barn is a barn." It's a stretch to place a rose and a barn in the same category. For one thing, the aroma sets them miles apart! But even though there may be a partial truth to the comparison, a barn is many things, as anyone who worked around one can verify.

A barn is wood and nails, bolts and nuts, steel and concrete. But a barn is more!

A barn is a shelter for animals and storage for farm produce. But a barn is more!

A barn is an early link in the food chain. It is the front door of the creamery…the genesis of milk and butter and the origin of ice cream. And over the objections of some, it is the doorstep of the meat packing plant…and steaks on the grill. But a barn is more!

A barn is the not-so-private boudoir for intimate animal relationships. Divinely ordained sexual unions happen as naturally and passionately as satisfying hunger at the manger and thirst at the water tank. But a barn is more!

A barn is a maternity ward for birth, a nursery for growth, a factory for turning animal fodder into human food, a hospital for curing disease, a home for the aged, a morgue for the dead. Barn walls witness the complete cycle of life, animal generation after animal generation. But a barn is more!

A barn is a fertilizer plant. Cleaning the gutters in a barn is made more meaningful when one realizes that the by-product of milk, butter and meat, nourishes the land. But a barn is more!

A barn is a meditation sanctuary. Performing certain routine chores that require simple repetitive motions…like milking cows by hand…offer a time for reflective thinking. Dad and Mom were masters at milking meditation! But a barn is more!

A barn deserves to be a thing of beauty. Just because it stinks is no excuse for it to be shabby. But a barn is more!

A barn is a hope for economic security. But a barn is more!

A barn is a thing of pride. But a barn is more!

A barn is the fulfillment of a dream. But a barn is more!

Most importantly, a barn is intricately connected with people. It is not an entity unto itself. It was built by people, used by people, owned by people. But a barn is more!

A barn is more than my pen can write!

Photos submitted by Donahue Sarff

Barns of Aitkin County Minnesota

Introduction/Overview   This project on locating and photographing older style barns in Aitkin County was initiated after hearing many comments about the decline and disappearance of barns from our landscape. This photographic record of the barns is an important part of preserving our Aitkin County history. Documentation of their presence was started in 2008. Since starting the project, quite a few barns have collapsed or have been removed by the owners. The majority of the barns were photographed from public roads with the rest being photographed where the owner has given permission either by verbal or written consent or when an adjoining landowner has granted permission (knowing that his/her neighbor would want their barn to be included). To protect the privacy of property owners no reference has been made about ownership in the road photographic section of this book.

Description of Barn Layout and Road Index   All barns are tied geographically to road numbers on major roads and general locations in Aitkin County. They were originally organized in a manner so photos appeared in the same order that you would see them while driving on a specified road. However, some areas contain township roads which branch off of the primary roads and also offer barn viewing opportunities. Due to the complexity of incorporating the secondary roads, they are tied to a primary road group and may not always appear in an expected order. The Barn Photo Road Index of each road will define the direction of the photos from north to south, east to west, or any other directions that occur. For example, Highway 169 photos begin by Mille Lacs Lake and terminate north of Hill City by the Itasca County line. This will simplify the complex combination of roads so interested parties can use the book as a "rough guide" to seeing the pictured barns with the understanding that many barns are not located on major roads. A general map of the major roads in Aitkin County was created to assist with a self guided tour. Some of the dead end roads which are often designated as lanes or places terminate in the yards of homeowners. **Please respect their privacy.**

Aitkin County Barn Photo Directions Index

Aitkin County Road 1 Begins in Aitkin and heads north and terminates at Aitkin County Road 3.

Aitkin County Road 2 * Begins in Malmo and heads east and crosses State Highway 65 and terminates at the Pine County line.
280th AVE (Lakeside), 210th AVE (White Pine)

Aitkin County Road 3 Begins in Esquagamah Township which is 14 miles east of Emily. It continues east and crosses Federal Highway 169 traveling towards Palisade. The portion from Palisade that terminates at State Highway 65 used to be State Highway 232 but is now part of the Aitkin County road system.

Aitkin County Road 4 Begins at State Highway 47 heads east and terminates at State Highway 65.

Aitkin County Road 5 * Begins at State Highway 47 approximately 6 miles east of Aitkin and heads north through Spencer, Kimberly, and Fleming Townships to Palisade. It continues north through Logan Township and terminates at Aitkin County Road 18. All barns that can be viewed from County Road 5 are listed as the first group of barns. There are numerous branches off of this road and they are grouped after those on the main road in the four previously named townships.

Aitkin County Road 6 Begins 5 miles north of State Highway 210 in McGregor, MN and terminates after 13 miles at State Highway 210 in Tamarack. 472nd ST (Haugen)

Aitkin County Road 10 * The Mississippi Great River Road begins 11 miles north of Aitkin off of Federal Highway 169 and continues and north until it terminates at the Itasca County line a couple miles north of State Highway 200. 340th PL, 290th PL 280th AVE (Logan), 590th ST (Verdon)

Aitkin County Road 21 Begins at the Mississippi Diversion Channel on Aitkin County Road 1 north of Aitkin. It is part of the Great Mississippi River Road continues east and north until it terminates at Federal Highway 169 just north of the Mississippi River Landing.

Aitkin County Road 11 Starts at the Crow Wing/Aitkin County line 3 miles west of its intersection with Federal Highway 169 at Bennettville. There are also barns to the east on 270th ST which splits to the north and south one mile east of 169. 435th AVE, 440th AVE (Hazelton)

Aitkin County Road 12 * Begins just west of the Mille Lacs Electric buildings east of Aitkin and heads south across the railroad tracks on County Road 12, turn left on State Highway 47 approximately 200 hundred feet and turn right onto County Road 12. Follow the road approximately 14 miles until it terminates at State Highway 47. 280th ST (Malmo), 295th ST Oriole AVE, 310th ST (Nordland)

Aitkin County Road 13 Begins approximately 5 miles south of McGregor on State Highway 65 just south of the Rice Lake NWR headquarters. Turn left at the convenience store and continue east 5.5 miles to the intersection with County 27. Turn left and cross the Soo Line recreational trail and make a right turn at Lawler and continue on 5.25 miles to the Carlton County line.

Aitkin County Road 15 The "Cedar Brook Road" begins approximately one-half mile west of the Security State Bank in Aitkin and continues west about 5.5 miles to the Crow Wing County line.

Aitkin County Road 16 * Begins in Lawler and continues north 9.5 miles to State Highway 210. Barns are also located on secondary spurs adjacent to County Road 16 in Clark and Salo Townships. 110th AVE, 422nd ST, (Clark), 395th LN (Salo)

Aitkin County Road 17 * Begins 1.5 miles east of the County Road 12 intersection with State Highway 47. It continues southeast approximately 6.5 miles until it terminates at State Highway 47.
320th ST, 350th AVE (Nordland) 370th AVE (Spencer)

MN State Highway 18 * Begins 3 miles north of the southwest corner of Aitkin County on Federal Highway 169 and continues along the north shore of Mille Lacs Lake to State Highway 47. After traveling south on State Highway 47 for 8 miles, turn left (east) on the second leg of State Highway 18 for 12.5 miles to State Highway 65. Continue east 10.5 miles until State the highway terminates at the Pine County Line. 230th AVE (Idun), 140th PL, 130th PL, 120th PL, 110th AVE (Wagner)

Aitkin County Road 20 Begins northwest of Shovel Lake 1.75 miles south of State Highway 200 at the west end of County Road 67. It continues south and east for 6 miles and terminates at County Road 19.

Aitkin County Road 22 Begins 3 miles north of Aitkin and continues west and north approximately 4 miles until it terminates at the Crow Wing County line.

Aitkin County Road 23/25 The Sprandel Road branches off of State Highway 18 on the line between Aitkin and Pine County and continues south about 1.5 miles to County Road 23. It continues west 2.5 miles to County Road 61 and north 2 miles to State Highway 18. County Road 25 begins 0.5 miles east of the intersection of the Sprandel Road and County Road 23 described previously. It continues south and west 3.75 miles to 100th Street which continues west 2 miles.

Aitkin County Road 26 Begins 4 miles south of the intersection of County Road 2 and County Road 38 one mile east of Malmo. It continues east 11 miles to the intersection with State Highway 65. It continues east and north about 8 miles until it terminates at County Road 2.

Aitkin County Road 27/State Highway 27 County Road 27 begins just south of Lawler and continues south 6.5 miles until it terminates at State Highway 27. State Highway 27 branches off of State Highway 65 at Jack's Shack and continues east 10 mile to the Carlton/Aitkin County line.

Aitkin County Road 28 Begins 3 miles west of the Aitkin stoplights on Highway 210. It continues south and east for 7 miles to Federal Highway 169. County Road 28 continues east 5 miles until it terminates at County Road 12. 310th ST and 465th AVE (Farm Island) 380th AVE (Nordland)

Aitkin County Road 29 Begins 4 miles west of the intersection of County Road 3 and Federal Highway 169. It continues north 11.5 miles to Swatara and another 7 miles until it terminates at State Highway 200.

Aitkin County Road 7	Begins in Swatara and continues east until it terminates at Federal Highway 169 near the Corner Club in Hay Point.
Aitkin County Road 30	Begins 3 miles north of Lawler on County Road 16. It continues west and south 7 miles until it terminates at State Highway 65.
Aitkin County Road 31	Begins 1 mile north of Tamarack on County Road 6 and continues north 3.5 miles until it terminates at County Road 64.
Aitkin County Road 32	Begins ¼ mile west of the intersection of County Road 6 and County Road 40 near Round Lake. It continues east for 6 miles to the Carlton County line.
Aitkin County Road 64	Begins 3.5 miles north of County Road 6 at the intersection of County roads 31 and 32. It continues north and west 9 miles until it terminates at County Road 14.
Aitkin County Road 38	Begins 1.25 miles east of State Highway 47 (Malmo) on County Road 2. It continues south 6 miles to the Mille Lacs County line.
Aitkin County Road 39 *	Begins 2.5 miles south of State Highway 47 on County Road 12. It continues south and east 4.5 miles until it terminates at County Road 12. 310th LN 450th PL Diamond Lake Street (Farm Island)
MN State Highway 47 *	Begins in Aitkin 0.5 miles south of the stoplights and continues east and south for 26 miles until it reaches the Mille Lacs County line. 292nd ST (Glen) 270th ST 240th LN (Malmo)
Aitkin County Road 53	Begins 3.5 miles east of State Highway 47 on County Road 4. It continues north 3.5 miles until it terminates at County Road 5. 350th LN (Kimberly)
Aitkin County Road 54	Begins at the entrance to the Aitkin County Fairgrounds and continues east and north until it terminates 6.75 miles later at Federal Highway 169. County 54N branches off on 395th Street and terminates at Federal Highway 169.
Aitkin County Road 56	Begins at the intersection of County Road 54 and Federal Highway 169 in Spencer Township. It continues east for approximately 8 miles until it terminates at County Road 5 in Kimberly.
Aitkin County Road 57	Begins 2.25 miles south of East Lake on State Highway 65. It continues east and south for approximately 9 miles until it terminates at State Highway 27.
Aitkin County Road 58	Begins at the SW corner of Idun Township and continues north 4 miles until it terminates at County Road 26.
Aitkin County Road 59	Begins 5 miles east of Country Road 38 on County Road 26 and continues 4.5 miles to the south where it terminates at State Highway 18.
Aitkin County Road 60	Begins 5.75 miles east from State Highway 47 on State Highway 18. It heads 3 miles south and splits to the west for one mile as Co Rd 60W as the initial Co Rd 60 terminates at the Kanabec County line one mile south of the split.
Aitkin County Road 9	Begins at the McGrath Forestry office just east of McGrath on State Highway 65 and continues west approximately 2/3 mile.

Aitkin County Road 61 *	Begins 1 mile north of McGrath on Highway 65. It continues east and south 11 miles until it terminates at County Road 23 two miles south of Giese. 170th ST 160th LN (Pliny) 150th LN 180th AVE (Williams) 160th AVE (Wagner)
Aitkin County Road 62	Begins 1 mile west of Highway 65 (McGregor) on Highway 210. It continues north approximately 8 miles until it terminates at County Road 3.
Aitkin County Road 63	Begins 1 mile west on County Road 3 from its intersection with State Highway 65. It continues north about 3 miles until it terminates at State Highway 65.
MN State Highway 65 *	Begins approximately 2 miles north of Jacobson at the Itasca/Aitkin County line. It continues south approximately 62 miles to the Aitkin/Kanabec County line. 190th AVE 657th ST 640th ST (Ball Bluff) 218th PL (Cornish) 610th ST (Verdon) 370th LN (Spalding)
Aitkin County Road 67	Begins 3.0 miles west of Hill City on State Highway 200 and 2 miles south on Aitkin County Road 29. It continues west 5 miles to the Cass County line.
Aitkin County Road 68	Begins 13.5 miles north of the intersection between State Highway 210 and Federal Highway 169. It continues 5.5 miles west until it terminates.
Aitkin County Road 74	Begins in Hill City and continues west and south until it terminates at State Highway 200.
Aitkin County Road 75/34	Begins 5 miles east of the intersection of State Highway 2 and State Highway 65. It continues south and east 7 miles until it terminates at Aitkin County Road 34. Turn left on County Road 34 and continue east 2 miles to the Pine County line.
Aitkin County Road 76	Begins 2.5 miles south of Aitkin County's stoplights on Federal Highway 169. Turn right and continue south 3 miles until the road intersects with Federal Highway 169 again.
Federal Highway 169 *	Begins approximately 2 miles north of Garrison and continues approximately 63 miles north to the Aitkin/Itasca County line. 405th LN west 410th ST (Morrison)
MN State Highway 200	Begins 8.75 miles east of Jacobson at its intersection with State Highway 2. It continues west approximately 24 miles to the Aitkin/Cass County line after passing through Jacobson and Hill City. 154th PL (52-22) 250th AVE (Verdon) 340th AVE (Quadna)
MN State Highway 210 *	Begins at the Aitkin/Crow Wing county line 5 miles west of Aitkin stoplights. Continue east 8.5 miles on Federal Highway 169 to the intersection with the eastbound segment of State Highway 210. Continue east 14 miles to McGregor and another 12.5 miles to the Aitkin/Carlton County line. 405th LN east off of 169 to 340th AVE Morrison 270th PL (Jevne) 185th PL 420th ST (McGregor) 150th AVE 140th AVE (Clark)

*Primary roads which have an extensive amount of secondary roads where barns are located. The major secondary roads are listed after the description.

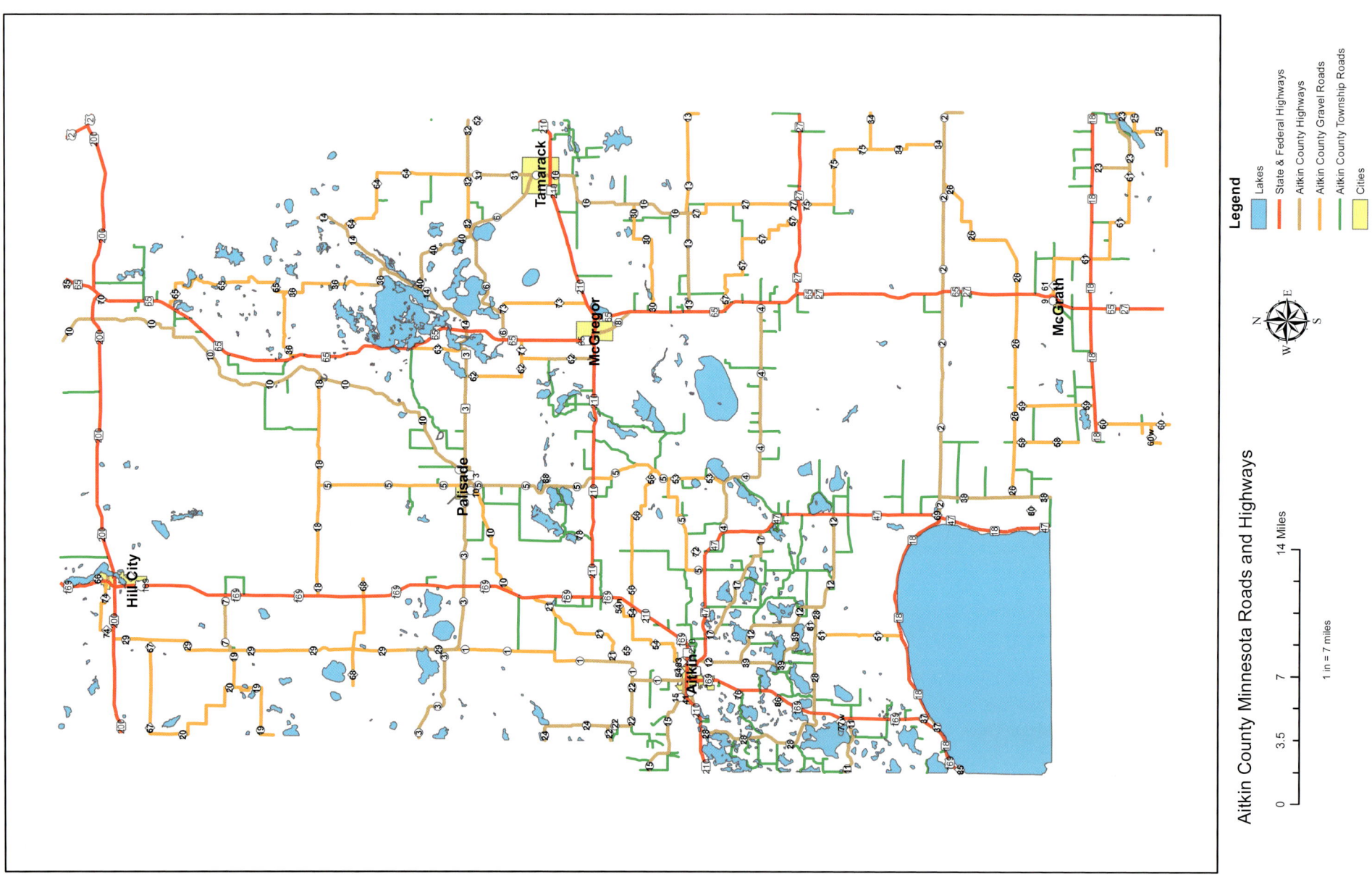
Aitkin County Minnesota Roads and Highways

County Road 1

Down

County Road 2

County Road 3

Collapsed

Down

Down

Down **Down**

Down

County Road 4

Century Farm - 1901

Down   **Down**

County Road 5

Burned

County Road 5 - Logan Township

Down

County Road 5 - Fleming Township

County Road 5 - Kimberly Township

Century Farm - 1905

County Road 5 - Kimberly Township

County Road 5 - Spencer Township

Collapsed

County Road 6

29

County Road 10

Century Farm - 1893

County Roads 10 and 18

County Road 11

Down

Down

County Road 12

Century Farm - 1908   **Century Farm - 1905**

County Road 13

County Road 15

Century Farm 1888

Collapsed

County Road 16

Century Farm - 1898

Century Farm - 1883

County Road 17

State Highway 18

Down

County Road 21

County Road 22

Century Farm - 1908

County Road 23

County Roads 23 and 25

Down

County Road 26

County Road 27 and State Highway 27

                      Down   **Burned**

County Road 28

Down

Down

County Roads 29 and 7

County Road 30

County Roads 31 and 32

County Roads 32 and 64

Down

County Road 38

County Road 39

State Highway 47

Century Farm - 1894

Down

County Road 53

County Road 54

County Road 56

Century Farm - 1900

County Road 57

County Road 58

Collapsed

Century Farm - 1893

County Road 59

County Road 60

County Roads 9 and 61

County Roads 62 and 63

State Highway 65

Down

Collapsed **Collapsed**

County Roads 20, 67, and 68

County Road 74

County Roads 75 and 34

County Road 76

Federal Highway 169

Down

Burned

Down

Century Farm - 1906

State Highway 200

Down

State Highway 210

Down

Down

Minnesota Century and Sesquicentennial Farms in Aitkin County

Century Farms
The Minnesota Farm Bureau and the Minnesota State Fair work in conjunction on the Century Farm program to honor Minnesota families that have owned their farms for at least 100 years are at least 50 acres in size and are currently involved in agricultural production. Since the program began in 1976, around 9,500 farms in Minnesota have been recognized as Century Farms, with roughly 250 farms being designated each year. The Minnesota State Fair designates Century Farm status in early summer of each year. Century Farm families receive a commemorative sign, as well as a certificate signed by the president of the State Fair, president of the Minnesota Farm Bureau and the Governor of Minnesota. centuryfarms@mnstatefair.org

Sesquicentennial Farms
Minnesota Farm Bureau also honors Minnesota families that have owned their farms for at least 150 years are at least 50 acres in size and are currently involved in agricultural production.

A commemorative certificate signed by the Governor of Minnesota, commissioner of Minnesota Department of Agriculture and president of the Minnesota Farm Bureau Federation will be awarded to qualifying families, along with an outdoor sign signifying Sesquicentennial Farm recognition

Name	Year	Township
Paulson, Albert Lloyd	1883	Nordland
Wasserzieher, Kenneth W.	1884	Hazelton
Damar Homestead Farm	1887	Lakeside
Dotzler, Donald B.	1888	Aitkin
Kullhem, Burton and Tambrey	1893	Workman
Thomsen, Agnes	1893	Idun
Howard, Lawrence and Betty Ann	1894	Kimberly
Boyes, Gene and Maureen	1898	Clark
Field, Marvin W. and Laverna	1900	Rice River
Hanson, Edwin and Yvonne	1901	Lee
Obernolte, Donald E. and Leann M.	1901	Shamrock
Schatz, Wendy L. and Alan B.	1901	Shamrock
Bertrand, James and Michelle	1903	Jevne
Robert Hillman Family	1905	Nordland
Nelson, Thomas and Roland	1905	Davidson
Biskey Family Farm	1906	Macville
Alleman, Richard and Jennette	1908	Wagner
Hyovalti, Les and Yvette	1908	Nordland

Information & Sesquicentennial sign reprinted with permission from Minnesota Farm Bureau
Century Farm sign reprinted with permission from Minnesota State Fair

Styles

There are many different styles and shapes of barns located in Aitkin County. A few of them are shown on this page.

Conditions

The conditions of barn varies greatly in Aitkin County and many have collapsed in the past few years.

Foundations

The barns of Aitkin County have a variety of foundation types as shown on this page.

Split Field Stone

Homemade Cement Blocks

Concrete Floor

Bare Dirt

Poured Concrete

Brick

Concrete Blocks

Brick

Winter

Winter often offers peaceful opportunities unlike any other season due to the blanket of snow covering the ground

**Many barns were surrounded by an assortment of outbuildings.
Corn cribs, chicken coops, and outhouses were commonly found.**

There are many unique interior and exterior features found on older barns around the county.

Farming equipment of days gone by

And the sentries stand alone, watching always watching, keepers of long ago secrets.

The Barns are Standing

Maintenance

Maintenance is extremely important to maintain the quality of a barn. Replacing the roof, repainting the exterior and shoring up walls or the frame work are common activities.

HULIN BARN

Built in 1910 the top half is from the first Aitkin County Fair grandstand. The bottom is constructed with railroad ties.

In 1928, a cement floor was poured for the cost of $3,000. At that time, it was considered an experimental barn because farmers were unsure how cows would react to a cold floor. Straw was used for bedding to help insulate the floor thus allowing a better milk production.

Story submitted by Norman Hulin

TARR BARN

The barn was built in either 1942 or 1943 by my father and mother in-law, Virgil and Lillian Tarr. Ralph Beneke's parents, Paul and Justine Beneke, were renting the farm when the barn was built.

Ralph and his twin brother Robert painted their initials in green paint, in the haymow. They are still on the walls—R.B. and R.B.

The barn is no longer used as a barn but as a garage and storage.

Story submitted by Florence Tarr

LIND BARN

This barn was built for O. J. Lind (Gust) in 1927 by local carpenter, Chris Christiansen of Palisade. Lumber for the barn was purchased from Keath's Sawmill and hauled by horse drawn wagons to the building site.

The barn was used for dairy operation, until switching to beef operation and is still in use for farming today.

Story submitted by Don and Hulda Lind

ROSEBERG BARN

Original owner, Elof Roseberg, my Grandfather replaced an earlier log barn with this barn he built in 1928 from home sawed lumber.

During construction, a wind storm blew down the rafters after they had been set and tacked in place. The neighbors came the following day and put them up again. The rafters are laminated from 1" boards which were sawn on a curve in a special jig. The haymow floor joists are tamarack logs slabbed off on 2 sides to 6" thickness. The neighbors told my grandfather that he could store a locomotive in the hayloft.

Cows were housed and milked in the barn until 2008. Now the barn is used for storage and hay is stored in the loft.

Story submitted by Robert Roseberg

GOBLE BARN

The barn was built mainly by Louis Guenther in 1928 with minimal help. The barn was built mostly with salvaged lumber from Lake Esquagamah, tamarack and cedar from the farm.

There was a water holding tank, fed by gutters from the roof and well, giving the cows a constant supply of water to their drink cups. Manure was taken out in a 2' x 4' bucket attached to a pulley system. The barn was built into a hillside. The haymow door was ground level on the west side allowing wagons to be driven in. The doors to the milking floor were on the north and south sides, ground level but one story below the haymow. The barn was considered very modern and innovative in 1928. There were two air vent shafts that ran from the milking level to the roof. The mangers were cement. The original stanchions had a group tract with four or five opening with one lever.

Story and photo submitted by Fahma Goble

BARNS owned by CLIFFORD R. and GRACE JOHNSON
BRYAN J. and CHRISTINE C. BAILEY

Located in Nordland Township this barn was built in the late 1940s by Andrew "Dave" and Anna G. Olson. It is 32 x 50 with cement block walls. The roof of the haymow was sheeted with aluminum panels. Many times over the years the roofing needed to be renailed. Fritz Lueck remembers doing it during the '50s. The Olsons raised Guernsey cattle.

Victor "Luverne" and Catherine M. Sjodin bought the farm in 1955 and continued to raise Guernsey cattle.

In June 1962, Bryan J. and Christine C. Bailey moved onto the farm. They bought the Guernseys and brought a few Holsteins with them.

January 1963, Clifford R. and Grace Johnson bought the farm and contracted it to their daughter and son-in-law, Bryan and Christine Bailey. The Baileys continued their dairy operation until 1990. They added a milk house in 1971 and started shipping bulk milk. Stanchions were replaced with tie-stalls and a calf shed was added. The Baileys became owners in 1977.

The Baileys had early summer barn dances for a few years in the '60s. John Pearson painted the barn. He balanced a long ladder on the peak to reach the trim boards. In 1999, the roof was repaired and again in 2003 when we had it painted.

October 2007, David M. and Elaine A. Pearson purchased the farm. The barn is not in good shape but still standing over 60 years.

Clifford R. and Grace Johnson built this barn around 1940. They used this barn for their dairy operation for over 20 years. They got electricity in about 1943 and a milking machine about three years later.

They sold the farm in 1971. It is now owned by Larry and Jackie Wagner. The barn has been torn down.

This barn was used for the dariy operation of Cecil and Esther Spaid. There was a hay shed with lean-tos on each side for cattle.

Bryan J. and Christine C. Bailey purchased this farm in 1957 to begin their dairy operation. They sold it in 1963. The property is now owned by Stephen and Carol Reinhardt for pasturing beef cattle. The barn has been gone for a long time.

Story and photos submitted by Christine C. Bailey

BERNDT BARN

This barn was originally built by Charles Niemi in 1950. The barn was added on by Rueben Niemi

We are still in the farming industry.

Story and photo submitted by LouAnne Berndt

DOUG and MAVIS OLSON BARN

This barn is located in Bennetville, Hazelton Township. To our knowledge it was built in the early 1940s. It did not have a silo at that time.

In 1982, construction began to convert the barn into a house. A silo was acquired from a neighboring farm. It was taken down, moved and reconstructed, and attached to the barn creating an entrance.

Story and top photo submitted by Doug & Mavis Olson

HORNIG BARN

The barn was built in 1930 and was located on the shore of Wilkins Lake. Iva Butcher purchased the farm in 1947 and had the barn moved to its current location. She had milk cows until 1975. We purchased the property in 1984. We raised horses up until 2011. We now have two goats and one sheep.

Story submitted by Gary & Sandy Hornig

BUTENHOFF BARN

This is the original dairy barn of the Monson farm south of Aitkin, in Nordland Township. It was built sometime between the years of 1905-10. I have done quite a bit of restoration to keep it sound, but the most beneficial addition was who ever put the tin on the roof some 50 years ago.

Story and photo submitted by Chuck Butenhoff

VIC and LOMA PETERSON BARN

This is a picture of barn construction during the summer of 1932 on the farm owned by parents, Victor and Loma Peterson, located in Section 24 of Clark Twp. The completed barn picture was taken in November 1939.

Story and photos submitted by Gary Peterson

JOHNSON BARN- Idun Township, Section 5

This barn belonged to Hans & Martha Johnson. Since 1977, has been owned by Roger and Joan Gerhardson. It has fallen down now!

Story and photo submitted by Joan Gerhardson.

Gene and Maureen Boyes
Century Farm – 1898
Clark Township

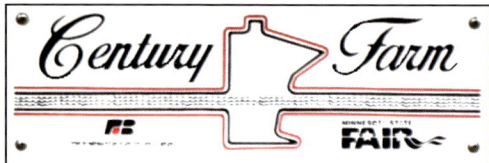

Western Style Barn painted red and white

This was the second barn built on this place in about 1920 by a local builder, Charley Gustafson. It was struck by lightning in August 1946 just after we had filled it with hay, and it burned to the ground.

This log barn is the first barn built on this place in 1898, probably by Jay Clark and John Maxwell, two trappers who were handymen. The shed barn built on the south end was added later. Note the split cedar shakes on the old log barn roof. These old wood shakes are in better condition than the wood shingles on the shed.

This is the third barn built on this place. It was built approximately in 1950 by a local builder, Walter Nelson. We are the original owners of the barn and are no longer in the farming industry. We use our barn for storage.

Story and photos submitted by Gene Boyes

NIESEN BARN

The original owner of this farm was Alex Fredrickson who purchased the place in 1915. The farm was purchased by Fred Pierie in 1973. Sometime between 1973 and 1977, Fred built this barn.

The original house that Alex Fredrickson built was removed in 2004 when we built our home.

The barn is of solid build. We have hogs in the barn and store hay bales in the loft. We intend to re-roof and re-side the barn to keep it in a sound state.

Story submitted by Jacob Niesen

SWANSON BARN

This barn is on property nine miles southeast of Aitkin which was originally owned by Arthur and Nannie Swanson. It was constructed in 1935. Alex Swanson, a brother, was the primary carpenter. Elof Green (Nannie's brother) sawed the bulk of the lumber from logs off the farm. Some of the main timbers were hewed. It has a poured cement foundation and floor. The exterior walls and roof were covered with galvanized tin. Friends and neighbors provided labor in exchange for services to them.

The barn dimensions are 42' by 32'. Originally there were stalls for twelve milk cows plus a team of horses with space to spare. The haymow equipped with a carrier and fork for moving hay held enough hay for one-third of the winter. During the mid 1940s, electricity became available so water was pumped to drinking cups for the cattle. The water pipe from the well to the barn can be seen in the picture.

The sturdy construction with some minor repairs has preserved the building so it is even usable today.

Story and photo submitted by Elwood Swanson

HASSELIUS BARN

Andrew Hasselius bought the home and 40 acres in 1893 for $600.00 from Duluth Central Railroad. It was paid off in 1902.

The barn was built in 1934 by local farmers. This replaced an older barn. The cows were sold in 1971 thus ending the barn being used for farming. It is now used as storage with the acreage farmed by locals.

Story submitted by Bruce Hasselius

SHARP BARN

Robert Sharp, owner was helped by neighbors and his brothers in the 1920s to build this barn. The family farm has remained in the Sharp family since then. My Grandfather Robert's hard work has lasted a long time.

The dairy cows were sold in 1958 and we stored small bales of hay inside until the early 1990s. There was a wooden stave silo which was taken down in the 1950s.

The barn was built from wood cut on the farm. Back in its day it held barn dances. My sister and I learned to roller skate in the haymow – early 1950s. Robert Sharp's great-great grandchildren had Easter egg hunts in the haymow. As it is no longer safe to enter, Robert Sharp's great-great-great grandchildren are allowed to step in carefully so they can see why it is no longer safe for them to enter.

Story submitted by Sylvester & Marion Klous

JOHNSON BARN – Rice River Township

The Johnson family is the original owners of this farm with Jalmer Johnson building the barn in 1929.

The west side was built first, using hand hewn logs that were originally used for a house. The house was located several miles away, somewhere east of Jack's Shack along County Road 27. The house was never completed but was dismantled and moved here to build the dairy barn. The hay was stacked outdoors for several years on the east side until the haymow was completed. The east portion was added for beef cattle in 1973. Dairy operations stopped in 1958.

Arnie Johnson purchased the farm from his father, Jalmer in 1971. Eric Johnson bought the farm from his father in 2001.

The original wood lap siding was replaced with sheet metal in 2009 and structural repairs made to the barn to prevent it from falling down.

Story submitted by Eric Johnson

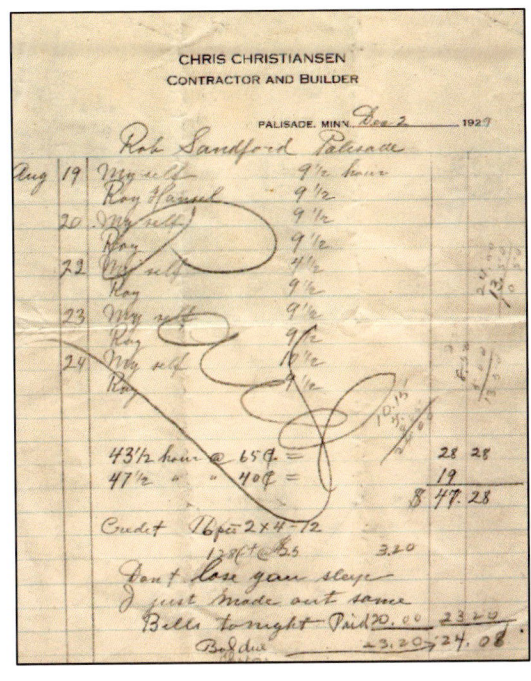

SANFORD BARN

My father, Robert Sanford, had the barn built the year I (Audrey) was born. It was built the summer of 1929 by Chris *"Carpenter"* Christiansen. It was the last barn he built and he said it was the best.

This was not the original barn on our homestead as my father had a temporary barn for a few years.

We belonged to a Woodcarvers Club that met and camped at the farm every fall for many years. We used the barn to sit in and carve evenings. The barn still holds some of the carving projects.

I found the ledger listing all the costs – several pages listing every hinge and board and hours of labor. The total cost looks like $1,219.76.

Story and photos submitted by Audrey Engels

PYNE BARN

The Pyne farm was originally homesteaded by the Villineau family. The barn was built by a Swedish immigrant named Oscar Melvick who came to this country in 1912. Melvick's first project upon arrival to Aitkin County was to harvest the trees on this property for beams to build the barn.

Story submitted by Jonathon Pyne

GRIMSBO BARN

My father, Ben Grimsbo built the barn in about 1920. My family is the original owners of this property and barn. We are no longer in the farming industry but use the barn for a garage and wood shed.

Story submitted by John Grimsbo

KRUSE BARN

This barn was built in 1915 by Dave Tweedy and his brothers, Levi and Albert. Our family is the original owners of this property. In 1968 we held a wedding dance in the barn.

Story submitted by Barb Kruse

McKAY BARN

A family by the name of Holmes from Ottumwa, IA built this barn in 1903. They were the second homesteaders to this property. It originally had a silo but was torn down in the 1940s. There are cedar shingles underneath the sheet metal which was put on by "Greasy" Tibbetts. It is no longer used for farming but as storage with 90% being junk items.

Story submitted by Don McKay

WEBBER BARN

This barn was built in 1938 by Henry Erickson and neighbors. There was an old smaller barn where the lean-to is.

We are in the process of restoring the barn to original. So far we have had the west wall straightened, the roof straightened, and a new post in bottom of barn to straighten the floor. We use the barn mainly for storage.

Story submitted by Thomas & Audrey Webber

CREIGHTON BARN

This barn was built about 1936. It was moved to this location in 1960 by the Booker family.

We use the barn for storage purposes.

Story submitted by William C. Creighton

PAULSON BARN

Erland and Elsie Paulson bought the farmland that this barn is on in either 1954 or 1955. Located in Spencer Twp, Harry Johnson son of Oscar Johnson owned the property.

Story and photo submitted by Elsie Paulson

FLOYD HOGAN BARN

The barn was built about 1946 by Paul Hyytinen and Floyd Hogan. The herd of Carnation Holstein cattle housed in this barn was Aitkin County's highest producing herd in the 1950s.

The farm is now owned by Jerry and Cherie Holm.

Story submitted by Cherie (Hogan) Holm

DAVIS BARN

The original owners were Lloyd and Leona Davis who started building the barn in 1958 (the block walls) and was completed in 1959 (the haymow). It is 32 feet wide by 60 feet long and has 26 stanchions. The cost of the barn is unknown but Lloyd and Leona did as much of the labor as possible themselves. Paid laborers were local men: Magnus Westling, brother-in-law, Arden Ray, neighbor, and Vernon Westerlund, neighbor. Melvin and Evelyn Davis, brother and sister-in-law, helped with the farming (haying) while the barn was being built. Charlie May, a bachelor farmer and friend of the family did volunteer labor and financed the barn. Charlie raised registered Holsteins. Charlie lived to be 107 years young.

Lloyd Davis retired from milking cows about 1973, but maintained a herd of young stock for a number of years. The barn is used by family for storage.

Leona Davis passed away in 1981 and Lloyd Davis passed away in 2008 at 97 years of age.

Story and photos submitted by Diann Hendrickson

MAZNIO BARN

This is the original barn on this property and was built in 1920 by Walter Richards. The main structure is made with wooden pegs instead of nails. It is made with mostly poplar wood.

This farm has been in our family for about 55 years.

Story submitted by Joseph Maznio

JOHNSON BARN – Tamarack

The barn was built in 1929 by my father, Elmer Johnson. In the fall of 1932, lightning struck the barn burning the building except for the eight foot concrete base. It was rebuilt by my father, Elmer Johnson, and friends and neighbors. The barn is still in very good condition with three additions to the original barn.

The barn and property is still in the Johnson name. We use the barn for hay storage and small equipment storage.

Story submitted by Melvin Johnson

SARFF BARN

This photo shows the Sarff barn under construction at an important stage. During the summer of 1948, we completed the construction and raising of rafters. And by *"corn tassel"* time, we had most of the roof boards on. The temporary bracing is holding the upper structure ready for siding…and the permanent cross-bracing. The scaffold used for the installation of the hay carrier track is still in place. I can see and remember so much more. It is difficult to describe my own personal emotions when I see this photo. It helps me remember the sense of accomplishment when we arrived at this stage in the construction. It really is beginning to look like our new Sarff barn!

Story and photo submitted by Donohue Sarff

BLOMBERG BARN

Marvin and Donna Borgman first built the barn on their farm in Section 30, Spencer Township located over by the old dump grounds. They purchased property in Section 20, April 22, 1959 from Myrtle Bartles and sold the Section 30 property on May 16, 1962 to Basil LaBlanc. Between 1959 and 1962 the Borgmans took down the barn in Section 30 board by board, and rebuilt it on the Section 20 property. When the Borgmans owned the property, they had about 20 cows of which they milked 12-14 cows. The barn size was 14 x 40 with a 14 x 40 addition.

After the Blombergs purchased the property in 1976, the barn was beginning to lean a lot. Harvey Blomberg with the help of his father-in-law, Alvin Thorne, straightened the barn up in 1977. The Blomberg family used the barn for hay storage, horses, and a Shetland pony for a number of years. Presently it is used for storage.

Story submitted by Judy Blomberg

THOMSEN BARN

The farm was homesteaded in 1893 by my Grandfather, Cornelius Mandius Thomsen. Cornelius built the barn in 1922 using White Pine lumber from the farm. The barn was used for 68 years with milk cows and beef cattle.

The barn is located on the west side of Bear Lake. On the right side of the barn there was room for nine cows and on the west side there was room for six cows and a team of horses. In the middle of the barn, there was a walk way to the other side which would house the young stock. The hay mow was just behind and on the top of the walkway.

The farm was passed down to my Father, Thoralf T. Thomsen and my Mother Agnes. It was then passed down to the four children in 2008. The barn is still standing in 2012.

Story and photo submitted by Conrad Thomsen

The Barn with a Star
Story (written 1991) and photo submitted by Sara Jane Johnson McCormick

It was a warm summer evening as we walked to the barn for chores on the slightly worn path from the house that crosses a little ditch by way of a single board bridge. The red barn had a white star on the hayloft door that my grandpa had made out of wood slats. I could always tell we were close to Grandma's house when I could see the big star.

I reached the barn ahead of Grandpa and Grandma, but, being only six, I couldn't open the heavy door that slid on a track, so I had to wait. After Grandpa opened the door I hurried in to beat the big black dog with golden circles above his eyes, but Bubbles didn't want to come in second so he just pushed me out of the way and bolted through the door.

The barn had an uneven cement floor with shallow gutters that my grandpa had poured himself when they built the barn. The supports that ran from floor to ceiling were logs six to eight inches in diameter. The barn smelled of cow manure, sweet dry hay, and old wood, two silver milk cans sat against the wall beside the door to the milk room where pails were washed and milk was kept after the cans were full. The stainless steel sink gleamed and the steamy water and smell of Hilex and soap gave the milk room its air of cleanliness.

I went around opening all the stanchions and putting a scoop of feed in front of each stall. When I finished, Grandpa swung open the back door and called "Come boss," and the black and white cows that had been waiting behind the barn to be milked started to trot clumsily into the barn. Each cow knew exactly where she belonged and went right to that spot. I helped Grandma close the stanchions and patted each cow on the head. Grandpa and Grandma started milking by hand, first washing the teats and then milking a little milk into an old tuna can. It was my job to take the can to the middle of the barn floor and dump it into a dish that was made from the bottom of a Hilex bottle.

I went out the back door to find the goat. She was drinking from the stock tank where the water was always cool and refreshing when I ran my fingers over the smooth surface. Ornery noticed me and lifted her head from the water. Her dark beady eyes seemed to smile at me. I walked slowly towards the goat in order not to startle her. Ornery's big horns curled towards the back of her neck. As I started to pet her, she began to rub her horns on my stomach which tickled and made me laugh. Grandma cautioned me about being so close to the goat, but I knew Ornery wouldn't hurt me because she liked the attention I gave her.

Bubbles came around to the back of the barn. I left Ornery behind and the dog and I started down the cow trail. It led through a grove of hardwood trees, mostly elms and maples. The grass was short and the leaves were a bright green. As I walked, I sang little songs to myself and watched the ground for treasures I might find. The sun was starting to set and the sky was a hot pink, royal purple, and a bright orange as I hurried back to the barn.

I entered the back door and the sweet smell of milk greeted me. Grandma informed me that they weren't done milking yet, but in the hayloft there was a new batch of kittens that were big enough for me to go see.

I skipped to the ladder that led up to the opening in the ceiling. When I reached the top of the ladder, I looked around for the kittens, but I couldn't see them so I stood very still and quiet to listen for the mews of the baby kittens. I heard them in the far corner where about ten bales of hay were stacked. I tiptoed softly toward them not wanting to intimidate the mother cat. I picked up a tiny calico kitten with orange and brown patches. I held it only a few minutes, put it down, and picked up another kitten. After I had placed the last kitten back in its nest, I patted the mother cat one more time to reassure her that I would leave her alone to tend to her kittens.

As I jumped from the last rung of the wooden ladder worn smooth from years of use I saw that Grandpa and Grandma had just finished doing the last of the chores. We filed out the door and Grandpa pulled it shut behind us. We walked slowly back to the house. Grandpa and Grandma were tired from doing chores, and I was tired from a long day of play. When we reached the house, I looked back up to the barn in the pale light just after sunset. Its strong walls and roof seemed then to be everlasting and unchangeable.

The barn still stands on my Grandma's farm but things have changed greatly. It stands empty and vacant; no more cows or hay enter its doors, no more laughter and busy chatter bounce off its walls. The star that used to be a bright white is now cracked and gray from weather. When I see the barn now, it reminds me of my childhood, a time when my life was simple, and happiness was all around me.

LAINEN BARN

This barn was built in 1932 by V. William Lainen and his wife Ann using only a hammer and hand saw. It is located about two miles northwest of Tamarack on Cty Rd 6. The current owner is Kathy Sellers. She has maintained it. The roof line is as straight as the day it was built.

Story submitted by William Lainen, Son

ERICKSON BARN

The white barn on the late Beauford and Ruby Erickson farm is in Lee Township, Thor across the road from the Zion Lutheran Church. This is a Century Farm. The barn was built in the early 1920s by the Erickson family. As I remember, the only new roof (a tin one) was put on in the early 1950s by Dan Wilbur. Grandson, Doug Morris now lives on the farm.

Story submitted by Marlys (Erickson) Morris

OLESON BARN

The original barn on the property was small and made of logs. This barn was built in 1949 by brothers, Claude and Alvie Oleson, brothers. The star was designed and made by owner, Claude Oleson. The barn survived a tornado with little damage

The property has remained in the Oleson family. Lorraine Oleson, widow of Claude remained in her home until her death on November 25, 2012 at the age of 90.

Story submitted by Nels & Heather Oleson

HARDER FARM – taken in 1931

The farm house and barn were erected in 1909. The outbuildings came later over the years. My grandfather used a Montgomery Ward catalog plan for the house. The barn was built on an ad hoc basis. The farmhouse was remodeled in 1956, the barn reconstructed in the 1980s. It still stands today, easily viewed from State Hwy 210.

Story and photo submitted by Robert O. Harder

WEISS BARN

This barn was built in 1919 by Gustav Weiss with locally sawn Tamarack timbers and boards. It originally had shake shingles which were covered in the late 1940s with steel roofing. That was done by Erwin Weiss who had purchased the farm in the early 1940s. It was painted in the 1970s when the name **Chesley Brook Acres** was painted on the hayloft door. The old field stone foundation which is three feet wide is crumbling, but efforts are underway to reinforce the lower portion which was dug into the hillside. The barn is 28 feet wide and 40 feet long. It held 20 adult cattle or horses and 8 head of young stock. The hayloft was made to hold loose hay and later held 3,000 bales of hay which wintered the stock sufficiently.

Story submitted by Annamaria and Donald Weiss

VISNOVEC BARN

Painted April 14, 1975 by Patty McKinley for George Wilcox.

Submitted by Nicole Visnovec

CHUTE BARN

Russell and I were married on October 12, 1944. We set up farming on the land that was originally platted out with streets, lots, and alleys for the town of Hassman. We had this plat vacated back to farmland in 1945. We raised turkeys along with dairy cattle on this farm.

The barn burned on April 14, 1959. A passing by Fire Chief from Pengilly noticed our barn burning. He stopped and alerted us. The Fire Departments from Palisade, McGregor, and Aitkin responded. Many neighbors came to help put out the fire. We had a bucket brigade from the Rice River along with the fire departments. The women were in the house making coffee and sandwiches for the crew.

Russell had placed a board in front of the large end doors to keep the Rice River from entering the barn. The young stock were trapped on the inside. The men were trying to open the door to save the young stock when two young men from the Pick Family were passing by and stopped to help put the fire out. The younger man had just been discharged from the Marines. He told the men *"I don't want to sound like a know- it-all but I can open the door. Stand back."* With a running leap the young man was able to drop kick the doors open, saving the young stock. The barn was a loss but our cows and young stock were saved.

After the fire, we relocated our farming operation and our home to its present location where we had more acreage. This property is where my mother, Mary (Graton) Cartie lived with her parents before her marriage to Cyprien Cartie.

We had the basement and foundation ready for our Rice River house to be moved onto. A small bridge with iron trusses needed to be crossed. The house was too wide so they sawed it in two. After placing the house on the foundation, we found it had shrunk 1-1/2 inches in the move. At this time, we also built our barn.

In 1967, we added to the barn and silo (note the different colored sections). Russell and I earned the distinguished award of Aitkin County Farmers of the year in 1992 and were recognized at the University of Minnesota. We averaged about 50 milk cows. We added a Quonset barn to house approximately 35 young stock. In addition to the barns, we have a Coverall hay storage and a calf nursery.

In 1993, our son Phil and his wife Colleen purchased the cattle operation. In 2011, a dairy dispersal sale took place, due to a farm accident. Phil has a small beef herd. Their primary business is hay production and marketing that takes them into 17 states and 3 Canadian provinces.

I was the leader of the Lucky 13 4-H Club for 53 years. Russell passed away on December 4, 2009. We have five children. Our three oldest children attended Hassman Country School through the eighth grade. It was consolidated in 1963. Our five children are: Anne Schaak lives in Minneapolis, Theresa (Marshall) Hogenson lives in Prior Lake, Betty lives in Bloomington, John (Debbie Kingsley) who with his family lives on a beef farm in Morrison Township and Philip (Colleen Kent) and his family lives on the farm. I have nine grandchildren and six great grandchildren. I am still living in my original home.

Story submitted by Lucille Chute

Lucky 13

CARLSON BARN

My Dad, Albin Carlson came from Sweden in 1897 to Farm Island Township settling on the east side of Diamond Lake. My Dad built the barn in 1925. He towed the logs to build the barn down the Ripple River with a boat and an old Evinrude motor to the Simpsons sawmill.

I was the last Carlson to use the barn for milk cows. I milked cows up until 1983 at which time I sold the property.

Story and photo submitted by Donald C. Carlson

NORBERG BARN

The original owners were the Paakkonen family. Two generations of their family preceded us before we (Michael and Silvia Norberg) purchased the property in 1990.

The barn was built in the 1900s and is the original barn on this property in Cornish Township. This was a dairy stanchion barn into the 1960s or 1970s. A unique feature of this barn is the poured concrete walls. There are no concrete blocks used.

We now use the barn for hay and lumber storage.

Submitted by Michael Norberg

TOLVANEN BARN

The original barn on our family homestead was destroyed in a grass fire. This barn was built in 1925.

The barn was used for dairy cattle up to 1970. At that time we switched to beef cattle. The barn is now being used for miscellaneous storage.

Submitted by Marty Tolvanen

OLE'S RESORT BARN

This barn is located at Ole's Resort on Big Sandy Lake, McGregor (Libby), Minnesota. It was built in 1937 by Olaf Laursen. It was used for milk cows with all pasture and swamp around it to the river.

Ice chunks were stored in sawdust in part of the barn for ice boxes for resort cabins. State Highway 65 came through in the late 1940s and changed the river channel and terrain.

In later years, the downstairs was used for storage and the hayloft was made into a roomy apartment. Now it is used for storage.

Present owner is Rich Kusick.

Story submitted by Mary Kusick

NELSON BARN

The barn was built in 1929 for the Edward Hansen Farm. It is now the Nelson Farm.

Story and photos submitted by Roger & Anne Nelson

Sheeks Modern Dairy Barn to be Open to Public on Sunday

One of the finest new dairy barns in Aitkin County will be open to public inspection next Sunday afternoon, Oct. 3, at the K. W. Sheeks farm east of Kimberly.

Mr. and Mrs. Sheeks invite the public to call between the hours of 2:00 and 4:00 p.m. Free coffee and doughnuts will be served.

Measuring 36 x 60, the barn is made of concrete bricks, double walled to the eaves of a Gothic roof. Panels of glass bricks admit light and an automatic ventilating system maintains constant temperature inside the barn.

The haymow will handle 80 tons. Steel stanchions will accommodate 20 milk cows. There is also a maternity pen, a herd sire stall and calf stalls.

Concrete floor, air-line for the milking machine, and water cups at every stanchion are other important features.

Provision has been made for the installation of a power barn cleaner at a later date.

Adjoining the barn is a neat milk house, with concrete floor, built-in concrete cooling-tank, power water system, lavatory and shower bath. A room above the milk house is being finished off to serve as a "den" for the three Sheeks', sons Bradley 11, Jack 10, and Jerry 4.

Outstanding Guernsey Herd

The Sheeks' herd of 32 registered Guernseys dates back fifteen years, with the Langwater line of breeding being followed. During the past year, the herd averaged 438 lbs. of butter fat. One cow, 6-year-old "Evergreen Princess Genelle" produced 636 lbs of butterfat in 305 days, twice-a-day milking.

Since 1944, the Sheeks' herd has been a member of the Aitkin County Dairy Herd Improvement Association, with official testing records on each animal in production.

Present herd sire is a son of "Langwater County Squire", from the E. K. Gaylord herd at Oklahoma City, Oklahoma

The Sheeks' farm is the "old home place", where Mr. and Mrs. J. S. Sheeks settled in the pine forests 46 years ago. Now the pines are nearly all gone, and a 380-acre farm has been developed, with 100 acres under cultivation.

Mr. and Mrs. Sheeks, Sr., retired from active farming in 1943, and still live on the original homesite. "Ken" and his family live in a comfortable home a couple of blocks away, a stone's throw from Rice River.

It should be explained, perhaps, that in the Sheeks' family, modernization of the home preceded the building of the barn. Electricity, hot and cold running water, a "steel" kitchen, refrigerator etc., were all added to make the life easier for the lady of the household before the new shelter was blue-printed for the livestock.

Reprinted with permission from the Aitkin Independent Age September 30, 1948

KONSOR BARN

Present day owners, Ben and Barb Konsor are still in the farming industry using the barn for cattle and pigs. The haymow is full of hay.

Article and story submitted by Ben and Barb Konsor

JENSEN BARN

We got our place (known as the Viebahn place) in 1959 and moved there in 1962. The place had been vacant off and on for as long as 20 years.

The barn was in poor condition. Someone had stored square bales in the mow and did not pile them away – thus causing a part of the east side of the barn to break. We got a house mover with big timbers and equipment to repair it. We took down the stave silo as some seemed to think it was not safe. Historically that was maybe a mistake. We put up a new Westman silo and built one continuouous shed for a calf barn, shed over the barn cleaner, and a big sileage area by the big silo. Prior to that we built a milk house. We also put in a new cement floor along with a barn cleaner. I don't know when it was built as it was here when we came. It was 60 feet long. We always seemed to need more room. Art piled away the bales in the haymow and we also had a big hay shed for storing bales.

I have been through four major floods here.

Story and photos submitted by Pearl Jensen

DRAGOVICH BARN
Nordland Township

Mr. and Mrs. Paul Dragovich owned the farm until sometime in the mid 1950s when Paul died. We (Art and Pearl Jensen) attended their auction and were impressed with the farm. We lived on the place until 1962 when we moved to my present farm.

Robert and Ruth Koehler from Ohio bought it. It has changed hands a time or two until its present owners, Terry and Midge Johnson bought it.

I know very little about the barn. It housed about 20 milk cows and room for young stock. There was a round poured cement silo inside the barn besides the outside silo. It was a good farm but we always had a love for my present place.

Story and photos submitted by Pearl Jensen

CYPRIEN (PHILLIP) and MARY (GRATON) CARTIE BARN

The north section of the L shaped barn was built in 1912. The dairy section and the silo were added-on in 1925. The dairy section housed 30 cows with a haymow above. When I was about 12 years of age, I would walk behind a set of horses that would pull the rope that brought the hay from a wagon to the haymow that was locked to a track to the haymow. The hay would be manually pushed to the sides of the haymow. I would then unhook the rope from the horses' whipple tree and drive the horses back.

We also had a track that held a large manure carrier that carried the manure from the gutters out to a dumping stack outside to be used later on the fields as (natural) fertilizer.

We had a generator before the rural electrical lines were put in. The batteries were charged by a running gasoline engine. The generator would light the house and barn lights for two days before recharging was needed. We had a flowing well. We would pump water to an overhead tank that was over the calf pens. The water would then flow down the pipes to the cattle water cups.

The farm had a log barn before the double barn was built. To the west of the L shaped was another barn that housed the young heifers in the leantos and the rest of the barn was used for hay.

This barn and all the buildings including the house have always been kept in very good condition to this day. Wayne and Gabe Anderson, the current owners have a menagerie of animals.

H. E. and JULIA CHUTE BARN

This is the only building left on the Harold Edward and Julia Chute farm. The barn was built in 1939 with cement block foundation walls. H.E. was proud that he had a "hay maker" silo. The silo has rows of holes that would allow the loose hay to dry without fermenting. The barn housed dairy cattle. Another building on the farm housed machinery. It had an outside stairway that was used for the Morrison Township hall. H. E. Chute was an Aitkin County commissioner.

Stories submitted by Lucille Chute

MICKELSON BARN

In 1915, Ole and Ingeborg Mickelson purchased 80 acres in the SW ¼ of Section 9, Idun Twp for $4,000, moving in December from Clarkfield. Ole came first with the horses, cattle, and household goods; all in a railroad car. Ingeborg and the children came a few days later. At that time, the barn was a narrow, slant-roof building; later being moved and used for sheep housing.

In 1929, construction was started on a 36' x 56' barn, with a room addition called the milk house. The main floor walls were poured concrete, with wood above and a gothic style roof. The haymow, from the ceiling of the first floor to the peak was 28 feet. There was a 10 or 12' wooden silo built inside the barn, which was made of redwood tongue and groove, along with the floor of the haymow. In 1942, a cement floor, gutters, and stanchions were installed. Twelve stanchions and water bowls were shipped by rail from Albert Lea for a total cost $181. There was room now for milk cows, calf pens, young stock, and horses. The milk house had its own hand-dug well that Hans Johnson, a neighbor, dug.

In 1948, the wooden silo was traded to Westman Silo for $125 and a new 12' x 30' cement-stave silo was built on the east side. They took the wooden one out by cutting it into 6 foot sections and taking them out the haymow door. Westman Silo sold them for use as hog pens. A room was added, also, connecting the silo and the barn. Again, in 1988, the cement silo was taken down and a 16' x 40' one replaced it.

Ole deeded the property to his only son, Oliver in 1941 and in 1977 Oliver sold it to one of his sons, Stanley.

In 2001, Stanley sold the milk cows and started with beef cattle, so the barn was remodeled for nursing them, and Stanley's two sons, Ben and Russell, have taken over a lot of the work of farming.

1928 Barn

1930 Construction

Taken in late 1959

Story as told by Oliver Mickelson & Agnes Thomsen and written by Stanley Mickelson with photos.

LATVALA BARNS

The barn was built in 1939 by my Grandfather. The property remains in the Latvala name. The horse barn is older than the barn. We no longer use the barn for farming but use it for storage and as a woodshop. Grandpa always said, *"Stay out of the hay loft!"* ☺

Story submitted by Roland Latvala

LUECK BARN

The barn was built in 1905 or 1906 by Andrew Lundin. The barn was built about 200 feet south of where it now stands. In 1928, the County built County Road 28. The barn was on the section line and was moved north approximately 200 feet away from the section line to make room for County Road 28. W. E. Johnson and sons moved the barn to its present location.

The barn is 30 feet by 50 feet with mostly hand hewn framing. I put metal on it in the 1960s. I have owned the property since 1950 and now use the barn for storage.

Story and photos submitted by Fritz Lueck

SAMUELSON BARN

Although the exact date is unknown, to the best of our knowledge the Samuelson barn was built sometime between 1900 and 1910. The farm was purchased in 1899 and is located in Lakeside Township. It has remained in the family all these years. During the summer of 2013, the roof, siding, doors, and windows were replaced.

The barn is used from February to May to house beef cows when their calves are born each year. The hay loft stores 800 bales of hay/straw each year.

Story and 2013 photo submitted by David Samuelson

CHUTE BARN

When we purchased the property adjacent to our home, we inherited this barn. The barn was a tall barn with wind damage. We lowered the barn by placing the haymow floor onto the foundation. We replaced the roof with a metal one. The barn is sturdy and in need of siding. We now use the barn for storage of machinery and small bales of hay. On a corner of the barn is a carving by the previous owner that reads Jim Bird 1916.

Story submitted by Lucille Chute

BERG BARN

The barn was built in 1952. The Quonset barn (not pictured) was built in 1962.

Submitted by Jerry Berg

"Most Dramatic Rescue"
Category - Runner up
2011 Barn of the Year

David and Linda Hommes bought their Kimberly township farm on Camp Lake in 1988 and moved there permanently in 1991.

"Our preservation efforts began in 1988 when we shoveled out a foot or more of old pig manure to find the floor," Linda said. "Then with the aid of a tractor, David was able to straighten the barn. Plywood was then nailed to the side walls for support."

Over the years, lean-tos on the barn were dismantled. A "summer kitchen" which stood in the middle of the yard, was moved alongside the barn and became David's first shop. Soon, he'd outgrown the space and moved into the barn also. He added an outdoor wood-burning furnace, installed a steel garage door and replaced the old rolled roofing with metal.

In the interior, a new center beam was added to support the new tongue and groove plywood ceiling/haymow floor. The haymow now holds a 20' by 15' partitioned rack.

The barn was painted a rich Navajo Red to match the house and other outbuildings.

On the south end of the barn, a greenhouse was added and now houses a flock of bantam chickens and ducks.

"With the exception of replacing the roof," Linda said, "all of the labor was done by David, which I termed 'priceless'."

It cost the couple between $15,000 and $20,000 to complete the preservation.

*Reprinted with permission from
David and Linda Hommes and
The Aitkin Independent Age December 7, 2011*

> "The Friends of Minnesota Barns is a non-profit membership-based organization that actively supports efforts to keep traditional barns and other historic farm buildings part of the rural landscape statewide. (www.friendsofminnesotabarns.org)"
> Linda Hommes

ANDERSON BARNS

This barn is located on the Harold Anderson farm. It is estimated to be built in the early 1900s. The owner of the farm at that time was John Anderson. The barn's design was unique in the fact that the haymow was constructed in the mid section of the barn, extending from the ground to the highest point of the barn. The cattle were housed on both sides with easy access to the hay in the middle. This design was taken from the barns built in Finland, where John was born. It was used for milking dairy cattle until Harold built the new barn in the early 1970s.

Rueben Anderson built this barn in 1966 and 67. Its intended purpose was for milking Holstein dairy cattle. The contractor hired for the project was Leroy Nistler. Rueben was also assisted in building the barn by his twin brother, Harold. It was used for milking cows until 1986, when Rueben converted his operation to raising Simental beef cattle.

Harold Anderson built this barn in the early 1970s. It was used for milking Holstein dairy cattle. The contractor's name was Murdock, with Harold's twin brother Rueben also assisting in its construction. Harold continued to milk cows in this barn until the mid 1980s when he retired.

This barn is on the farm owned by Mike Anderson, who purchased the farm from Rueben Anderson in 2011. The barn is estimated to have been built in the early 1900s. It was built using logs and probably housed dairy cattle. A section of the barn was torn down in the mid 60s to accommodate a new barn with milk house.

Stories and photos submitted by Richard Anderson

ANDERSON BARN

This barn is on the Richard and Deb Anderson farm. It was built by Roy Anderson around 1970. His neighbor, Harold Anderson, and brother-in-law Gunnar Sundberg assisted Roy in the construction of the barn. Its intended purpose was for milking dairy cattle.

Story and photo submitted by Richard Anderson

BRYAN BARN

Knute and Ruth Holm owned this barn prior to current owner Lisa Bryan. The barn was repainted by Chuck Johnson who painted it red with yellow trim. The barn is now used for storage.

Story and photo submitted by Katy Johnson and Sara McCormick

BELL HORN RANCH BARN

This barn was built by Rueben Anderson in the 1930s when he lived there. It was a dude ranch with barn dances held in the 1930s. The barn is still used in the farming industry.

Story and photo submitted by Darrel Johnson and Sara McCormick

DAHL BARN

The barn was built in 1939 by Conrad Johnson age 65 and his son Alder age 25. It has 18" thick walls made of field stone and concrete. There is a copper steel roof and the cupola was designed by Conrad Johnson.

The inside has been remolded for boarding horses. The outer buildings are for hogs and chickens.

Story submitted by Greg Dahl

JARVA BARN

The barn was built in 1926. We use the barn for storage of yard equipment. Following is information we received from Edmond Jarva, the last of the Jarva children born (1928).

Simo and Aina Jarva were immigrants who came from Finland in 1899. They first lived in Hibbing where he worked in the ore mines as a machine operator.

In 1915, they moved to the Jacobson area where they built their farm on the banks of the Mississippi River. They had two eighty acre areas that were three quarters of a mile apart from one another. The farm prospered with hard work. No tractor only horses.

One of the pictures is of the thrasher crew thrashing oats barley and wheat – a community effort you can see by the family photo that the family grew to 13 children. My youngest sister and I were not yet born when the picture was taken. My mother worked hard with so many children and she had time to help with the milking chores by washing and sterilizing the cream separator every morning and evening.

Simo and my older brothers and the area itinerate carpenter put up all of the buildings. I treasure the boyhood life I had on the farm on the Mississippi River. I hope the owners of this farm and future owners will love this wonderful farm as I did. The Jarvas sold the farm around 1954. Good Luck to all who will live on this farm now and in the future!

Story and photos submitted by John Zigas

McQUINE BARN

The barn was built in 1904 and is the original barn on this property. It is currently a horse barn with hay storage.

Story submitted by Kevin David Will

"THE BARN"

Located in Spencer Township, the barn was owned by Fred Nyberg from 1951 to 1963 and Carl Schellin from 1963 – 1994.

Story and photo submitted by Carol Mills

HOGE BARN

Lars L. Anderson came from Sweden in the 1880s and homesteaded in Section 12 of Glen Township. He built the hand hewn square log barn soon after he settled there. Other families who have owned the farm throughout the years were E. J. Marvin, Albert Hanson family, Ted Reither family, Chester Hanson family. The property and log barn are currently owned by Kevin and Carol Hoge. The barn has now been converted into a deer hunting shack with sleeping quarters in the haymow. It is nicknamed the **"Thor Hilton"**.

Story submitted by Carol Hoge

HERMAN JANZEN BARN

Herman Janzen had Lemuel Insley build the barn for him in 1930. The working wage, during those depression times, was 30 cents an hour for a 10 hour day. The men were good workers and the barn was progressing so well that Herman gave them a nickel an hour raise!

Story and photo submitted by Debbie Janzen

JOHNSON BARN – HILL CITY

A carpenter by the name of Boleman built the barn in 1928. The original buildings on the farm include house, barn, garage, granary, and chicken coop.

We are the third owners of this farm. We have kept the farm in top shape. We used to sell milk to the town of Hill City and the barn is still used in the farming industry.

Story submitted by Henry Johnson

HOPPERSTAD BARN

The barn that is located on the farm owned by Kerry and Tracy Hopperstad was built in the 1950s. The owner at the time it was built was Ed Swanson. He, like most farmers at that time, had help from the neighbors during the construction stage. Cliff Sanbeck of Aitkin was one of those neighbors who helped build the barn. Cliff also said that his father, Art Sanbeck, and the neighbor across the road, Babe Salo worked on the barn.

The barn is still used today for our cattle and horses and the building is still in great shape.

Story and photo submitted by Kerry Hopperstad

1950s Flood – *Aitkin Independent Age*   Photo – *Mille Lacs Electric "Outlet"*

ZILVERBERG – HLIDEK BARN

Around 1916, Hans Petraborg of Aitkin built a barn on his farm northwest of town. Many of the boards and beams he used in the construction were taken from an old riverboat.

In 1936, the Jim Zilverberg family moved to the Little Pine Route farm. Mr. Zilverberg suffered injuries in a fall from the haymow in December of 1945 that he never recovered from, passing away in February 1946. His son, Jake still lives on the farm. He and his wife, Mary, milked cows in the barn until the mid 1960s, having as many as 50 cows at times. The barn was 48 feet by 72 feet and according to Jake, had room for about 70 ton of loose hay.

In the 1950s, Jake made some major repairs to the building, but by 1981, the barn was again in need of repairs, including re-roofing. No longer farming and not having a need for a building of that size, Jake decided it was time for the structure to go.

At this time, Dick and Darlene Hlidek of Minneapolis became involved with the barn. They own Old River Road Antiques, located along the Mississippi River northeast of Aitkin, and were in need of another building.

The project of tearing the old barn down was carried out by the Hlideks in 1981. Taking care to preserve as many boards as possible, they spent a total of 27 days on this process.

It was decided to scale the "new" barn building down in size to dimensions of 24 feet by 40 feet. The rafters were cut down proportionately so that the same roof line was maintained. All but half a dozen boards used to construct the new barn came from the original structure.

The Hlideks poured the floor in the fall of 1981, with the main structure being erected in the summer of 1982. The windows and finishing touches were added in 1983.

Story submitted by Dick and Darlene Hlidek
Reprinted with permission from the
Mille Lacs Electric "Outlet", August 1984

MORRIS-JOHNSON DAIRY

One of the most modern dairy operations in this area of Minnesota is the Morris-Johnson dairy farm, which is located about 4 miles SE of Aitkin on Hwy 47.

Richard Morris and Francis Johnson have been farming at this location since 1948. The farm itself consists of 880 acres. They lease several other tracts used mainly for a separate beef operation.

Last December (1967), "Open House" was held in their new 204 x 44 ft barn which has a new milk handling and storage room attached. This controlled environment barn is of the "free stall" type, which means that the cattle are free to move around inside as they please. Silage is automatically augured into the feeding bunk (located in the center of the barn) from the one 30 x 50 ft and the two 16 x 50 ft silos located just outside the barn.

When the cows are not feeding, they are free to "loaf" around in the long alleys on either side of the feeding bunk or they may bed down in the individual stalls next to the walls on each side. Each cow tends to claim her own stall as well as a certain position when she is feeding.

The automatic auger eliminates almost all of the back breaking hand feed distribution used on many farms yet today.

How is the milking handled? This is probably the most interesting part of the entire operation. One would think there would be confusion and disorder at milking time, but this is not the case.

The cows again tend to take their turn and sometimes even impatiently wait to get into the milking parlor attracted by a specially prepared feed ration which is automatically fed into each of the 12 milking stalls, which are arranged in a herringbone pattern, with six stalls on each side.

The actual milking is done by the man standing in the center pit, designed to eliminate bending over to install the milking machines on the cow. Lifting is also eliminated by the use of six "milking claws" which swing over into position under the cow.

Six cows can be milked at one time while the six on the other side of the pit are being prepared. When the six animals are done being milked, a gate is opened and the cows file out into the barn area and another six enter the side just vacated, all in an orderly fashion. Two men can easily milk 100 cows in about 2-1/2 hours.

The milk enters a pipeline from the machines and eventually ends up in a 1,000-gallon storage tank in the room attached to the milking parlor. There it awaits pickup by a bulk milk truck. This room or "milk house" also contains much of the modern, somewhat complicated looking equipment required in the operation of the milkers. The almost laboratory clean milk storage room and parlor are things you cannot help but notice.

How is the manure and other waste handled? An electric tractor pushes this material into ports provided in the alleys where it drops into three 53,000 gallon tanks which need to be pumped out about three times each year. Both hot and cold water are used to flush the floors of the barn, milking parlor, and milk house. When the storage tanks need cleaning, the liquid manure is pumped up and out into a large mobile tank which distributes it in the field where it is utilized as fertilizer.

The entire operation on this farm amazes anyone who compares it to the old methods still in use in many places.

Reprinted with permission from Marge Johnson and
The Mille Lacs Electric Cooperative, June 1968
Photos submitted by Marge Johnson

The Barns are Gone

Photo by Doug Blakesley

Photos courtesy of Aitkin County Historical Society - all photos dated 1931

WILLIAMS ROUND BARN

The round barn planned by Algot Williams and built by Algot and his sons, Gust and Gunner and young son Phillip was said to be the only round barn in Minnesota back then.

Algot's sons kept trying to convince him, they needed a barn for their cattle and so he said, *"If we need a new barn it will be different than any other."* He sat and drew up the plans and here is the round barn.

The stanchions were placed around the circle of the barn facing inward and in the middle was the grain shed. The stairway to upstairs was in the north side.

For many years the haymow was used for dances. The organ had to be pulled up on the hay ropes. Local people furnished the music.

The barn was built in 1912 and was still in good condition when it was pushed down by one of the families which owned it

Algot Williams lived there for a few years after his wife died in 1915. After that his daughter Anna and son-in-law Arthur Olson farmed, Phillip and Grace Williams, Signe Williams and Carl Olson lived there a short time. In 1930-31 because of the depression it was foreclosed on and the family lost it. From then on it was rented for years until finally a few families bought and resold it. Gaylord Westerlund finally bought the farm from the family who pushed the barn over.

This farm was remembered by many people as a stop off place for travelers during the days of horse and wagons or buggies, traveling on their way to and from Aitkin.

Story and photo courtesy of Aitkin County Historical Society

OCTAGON BARN

I do not know a whole lot about the barn. Most of what I know is second, third, or fourth hand. It was built somewhere around 1912 – 1914. I was told it was a Sears pre-fab kit when it was the Murrey and Anna Sutton farm. The Suttons held barn dances in it. The siding was cedar and it originally had a silo in the center where the cupola was. Edna Mahl told me it had a grain elevator that spiraled up around the silo that was always getting clogged, so they removed the silo and just had a large hole in the center that they threw hay down from the loft. It came down in the winter of 1977-1978 due to heavy snow loads. The Northern Productions Company (a business from the metropolitan area that resold barn lumber) in 1994-1995 cleared the collapsed barn.

Story and photo submitted by Shane Donohue

THOMPSON BARN

The barn was built in 1900 by the Sandy River Lumber Company. We believe they used it as a stable. The huge logs were cedar, the rafters and haymow floor long tamarack logs.

In October 1918, the forest fire came and burned the house and granary but spared the barn and another log building.

My Grandfather Frank Cleft purchased the property from the Lumber Company in March of 1918.

The barn blew down on July 4, 1999 when the Boundary Waters National Park was damaged. We used the barn for storage prior to that as we had quit farming in 1970.

Story submitted by Zola Thompson

PALISADE BARN

This barn is located on County Rd 3 halfway between State Hwy 169 and Palisade. It can be seen from the road. It is just north of the LP gas tank/station.

It was built in 1927 by the Father of Tex Bullis, a well known and liked person in the Palisade area. Tex would be in his late 90's if he was alive.

Different families have lived on the farm –Weston's, Clapp's, and I are the people I know of. I bought the place in 1979. The barn came down in October 2011 when Aitkin encountered the lowest barometric pressure recorded.

Story and photo submitted by Donald J. Christiansen

JACOBSON BARN

In 1911, John and Hannah Jacobson purchased a farm 3-1/2 miles east of Aitkin called the "Midway Farm" because it was halfway between their previous farm located on the Rice River and Aitkin. John, and his brother-in-law Peter Wohlin, and others built a new barn and other buildings. It flourished into a 60 head dairy farm which was one of the finest in Aitkin County. The farm was sold in 1919. The old Midway Farm was later purchased by Carl Gretchmann who lived there when the tornado of 1934 destroyed the barn.

Story and photos submitted by Jon Jacobson

MATTSON BARN

The land was purchased from Davidson McRae Stock Co. in 1910 by Axel and Sara Mattson. The original title goes back to Minnesota State Reclamation of Swamplands year 1877.

The current owners are their Granddaughter, Carrie Maalis and her husband Lynn Maalis. We do not know who built the barn or the date of the above photo. The recent photo shows the barn down with only the peak through the tall grass.

Story and photos submitted by Lynn Maalis

Long Gone Barns of southern Idun Township in Aitkin County

History and photo submitted by Gerald Wollum

TEMPLIN BARN

About a mile north of the intersection of Red Top Road (115th Lane) and County Road 60 on the right side of the road is the Templin place, which used to be the Old John Noraus place. A barn and a log house had been constructed by John Noraus in the early 1900s. The first school was held there in the house in the very early days. In 1920, William Templin purchased the farm and moved there from Hillman, Minnesota. He built a new, much larger frame house, and the old log house was sold and moved down the road south of the Soo Line railroad tracks.

On August 2, 1925, a Saturday night, Bill Templin's barn caught on fire. It started at about 7:30 p.m. in the haymow. Bill's oldest son, Chester, crawled in and tried to put out the fire but was unable to. He was nearly overcome by the smoke but was able to escape the burning building. The barn was a total loss. Not one to be put off, Mr. Templin began saving money and collecting materials. Late in the fall he held a barn raising, followed by a shingling bee in early December of 1925. In many cases in the early days, the only insurance you had was the assurance of help from your neighbors. The old farm is still in the Templin family. No photos of the old barn are known to exist, but the new barn still stands.

WOLLUM BARN

Further north along County Road 60 on the west side, just south of the Red Top Cemetery was the Art and Alice Wollum homestead.

Arthur and Alice bought 40 acres of some of the poorest land in Aitkin County back in the summer of 1912 for $11.00 an acre, and moved onto it in 1913 from Sioux Falls, South Dakota. Alice made the deal for the land, and commented about Red Top in a letter to Arthur *"...I am afraid you will be disappointed in the looks of Red Top. It isn't a patch on Sioux Falls. Only a station (small), a house*

The Old Barn at the Wollum Place in Red Top

and hotel combined, a schoolhouse at one side, and two or three houses." The next year Art built a small house and barn at the homestead. In 1917 after taking a job with the Soo Line Railroad, Art and his family rented a house in Red Top, and left the farm. They were unable to get anyone to buy the farm, and gave up and let it go back for taxes. The house and buildings burned in a forest fire, and only the concrete foundation remains today. No photos are known to exist of the barn.

In 1936 at their home in Red Top, Art built another barn using timbers salvaged from a demolished railroad bridge, obtained from the Soo Line. It was very much like a log building but the timbers just crossed on the corners. It was nailed together with six inch spikes. It was not on a solid foundation, and had mostly fallen down by the 1970s. Some of the old fir timbers that were not rotted badly were salvaged, and are still in storage.

MARTIN BARN

About a half mile west of County Road 60 on 115th Lane, was a farmstead built in 1912 by Phineas Nathaniel Martin, who moved there from Royalton. The barn that he built burned down in the early 1960s and a new one was built by Louis Randall, who lived there then. The new barn still stands, but the house burned in 1982.

OLSEN BARN

Martin G. Olsen homesteaded the NW quarter of Section 28 of Idun Twp in October of 1915. The Olsens actually started work on their homestead in the summer of 1914, and moved to it from Grantville in early September. It was a small farm located on a hill rising out of a peat bog swamp NE of the location of the old Soo Line gravel pit. It was reached via a corduroy road that crossed the swamp from the road that came from Jones Crossing. There was a small house atop the hill, and a barn set down into the hillside.

The Olsens were unable to eke out a living, and left the area in the 1920s. A couple of other people lived there over the next 10 or 12 years, but the buildings were abandoned when they burned down in a grass fire in the late 1930s.

JOHNSON BARN

Mrs. Emma Johnson's barn burned down in a fire in Red Top on October 2, 1939 along with a stack of firewood and M. B. Cater's tractor trailer rig. Fire crews from the area were on hand to fight the fire along with Ranger Anton Swedberg who brought one man water tanks.

WHALBERG BARN

The former O. W. Wahlberg farm south of the Soo Line grade along present day County Road 60 in Idun Twp had a good sized barn that fell down in the time around 1990.

KIRKEVOLL BARN

Along County Road 60 in Idun Twp about .9 miles south of Hwy 18 was the A. T. Kirkevoll farm, where a house and barn stood from very early in the 1900s until they were consumed in a fire.

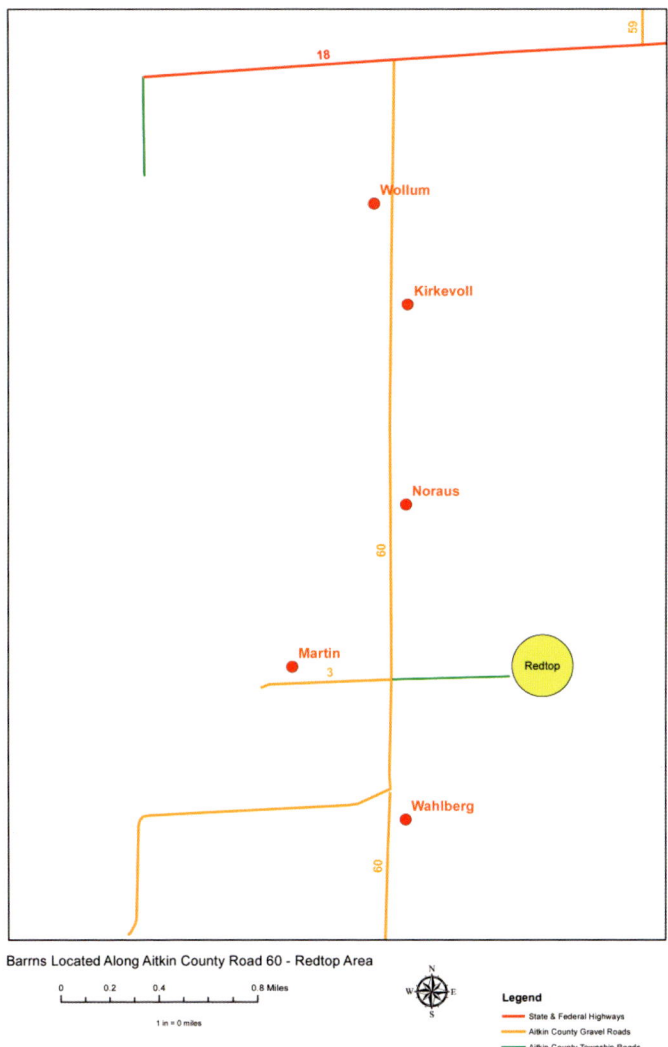

Idun Township map courtesy of Aitkin County Land Department

PURSI/ALANEN BARN

This 1919 barn was built in Salo Twp by my Finnish immigrant grandparents, John and Mary Pursi. They had settled in eastern Aitkin County in 1910, but lost their buildings, cows, and horses in the infamous 1918 Cloquet-Moose Lake forest fire. My always-optimistic grandfather, however, looked at the post disaster period as an opportunity to develop a modern *"American"* dairy barn. He began by securing a catalog from the James Manufacturing Company in Fort Atkinson, WI, one of the nation's largest producers of dairy barn equipment. Many of their products were developed and tested by University of Wisconsin agricultural engineers, who also recommended that farmers utilize gambrel-roofed barns to increase hay-storage capacity. The new barn, 50 feet long and 32 feet high, could house 20 cattle. It included water cups that allowed the cows to drink whenever they wished, metal stanchions, and a manure bucket that rolled along a steel track attached to the ceiling joists; most visible, and a constant delight to my grandfather, was the rooftop ventilator, topped by the silhouette of a cow and a wind direction arrow. Despite the barn's modern features, the hewn vertical logs used to build the lower story also gave it a distinctive *"Finnish"* appearance. (Vertical logs were employed since the tall trees necessary for horizontal log construction were destroyed in the 1918 fire.) Albert Oja, also a Finnish immigrant, served as the primary carpenter, just as he did for many other farmers who lived in eastern Aitkin and western Carlton Counties.

My parents (William and Ina Alanen) and I moved to the farm in 1950; the barn was occupied until the last cows were sold during the early 1970s. After a tornado destroyed the barn and some other buildings in 1978, I began to search for the rooftop cow and arrow. I found the twisted remnants in a tree, located about one-quarter mile from the original site. A blacksmith was able to straighten the bent metal, and today the feature is displayed in our Madison home. The cow and arrow always point east toward Fort Atkinson, the place where they were forged in 1919.

Story and photo submitted by Arnold Alanen, PhD.
Professor Emeritus University of Wisconsin-Madison

GM JOHNSON BARN

Located on the Tamarack River in Haugen Township, this barn was built by Gustav Martin (G. Martin or GM) Johnson in 1946. During the flood of 1950, the water almost came up to the barn.

The property was sold in 2002 to Tom & Dawn Johnson. The barn was torn down at that time.

Story and photo submitted by Darrel Johnson and Sara McCormick

Selected Aspects of the Economic History of Aitkin County, Minnesota
Introducing Less Well Known People and Events
II. Big Time Operators
Kenneth W. Sheeks, June 1968
Thesis for Master of Arts Degree – University of Minnesota, Duluth

Publication courtesy of Aitkin County Historical Society

The woodsy hills and slopes did have a degree of rich top soil, usually a few inches thick, which produced bountiful crops of grains and grasses when first farmed. Yields were comparable with those from good farm land elsewhere.[87]

Because of the shallowness of the top soil, the fertility was rapidly depleted. In a few years time the desirable varieties of clovers and grasses were crowded out by less desirable native grasses or weeds that could flourish on thin soil. Yields were down sharply. The rich, green verdant landscape gave way to pale, yellowish coloring. Something was wrong. Few farmers recognized the problem; fewer still took steps to correct the condition. Many gave up and left; hopes and dreams were shattered, as the neglected fences, forgotten fields, abandoned farmsteads attest.

That farming was difficult, that clearing the land of brush, stumps and stone was an overwhelming task is shown by annual reports of the County Extension office. In 1933 seventy-three per cent of the farmers did not raise enough feed to sustain their livestock. In some cases farmers had lived on the same land for twenty-five or thirty years and had only five or ten acres cleared and one or two acres under cultivation.[88] The successful farmers recognized earlier errors, corrected them, adapted their operation to existing conditions and created a solid economy based on the realities of the situation. Their activities will be noted later. There was another group that made history by the sheer flamboyancy, the magnitude, of their operations. Their efforts should not go unrecognized.

A. D. Davidson and A. D. McRae, who had been raised by Davidson, were land speculators from Sarnia, Ontario, Canada. Coming to Duluth, they incorporated the Davidson-McRae Land Company under a Minnesota charter in 1900. Mr. Davidson was president and McRae was vice president. They organized the Bank of Aitkin in August of the same year, again with Davidson as president, and McRae as vice president. Benjamin R. Hassman came to Aitkin soon after the bank was opened to become its cashier.[89]

The Davidson-McRae Stock Farm Company secured about five thousand acres of land, most of it in township 47, range 24, later named, appropriately, Davidson.[90] Called the Davidson McRae Ranch, it was intended as a major beef cattle operation. Headquarters for the ranch was established in magnificent stand of white oak on the northwest side of Rice Lake. Building sites were cleared and a complete set of ranch buildings erected.

The ranch house, a long, low structure in the true western style dominated the scene. Seventy-six feet long, it had quarters for the owners, the manager, cook, and housekeeper. There were also guest rooms. The den, or main rooms, had oak open beam construction with a massive field-stone fireplace. The ranch house burned down in the late twenties, but the fireplace continues to stand, although there is a new owner, the U. S. Department of the Interior.[91]

The other buildings were numerous. There was a bunkhouse and kitchen for about sixty men; a blacksmith shop for shodding the

---

[87] Pioneer Supplement, Aitkin Independent Age, Aitkin, Minnesota, June 28, 1951
[88] U.S. Dept. of Agriculture, Agricultural Extension Service, Annual Report, 1933, Aitkin, Minnesota p. 40
[89] Aitkin Independent Age, op.cit.
[90] Register of Deeds, Aitkin County, Davidson McRae Stock Farm Company, deed recorded in Book S of Deed Records, Feb. 21, 1901, p. 344
[91] "Personal correspondence of the author, letter from Manager, Rice Lake National Wildlife Refuge, McGregor, Minnesota, June 14, 1966"

horses, and building and repairing equipment. A large horse barn for twenty teams with a hay loft above, cattle sheds, hog houses, a granary, and similar structures filled in a ranch stead of several acres.

Crews were recruited to fence and clear the ranch. As many as 150 men worked at one time. The entire land holdings were completely fenced with barbed wire, even some very marshy, low acreage. Large fields, up to a quarter section in size, were cleared near the headquarters and put into cropland. Other lands were cleared and seeded with brome grass for pasture. Sixty years later much of these brome stands still endure. Leased from the government, they are cut for hay by farmers of the community.

A Mr. Nevis was brought in as manager of the Ranch. He stayed about ten years and then was replaced by a brother-in-law of Mr. McRae's, Wesley Hatley of Sarnia. By this time (1912) the owners realized that they had a losing proposition and were merely keeping the place going until they could find a buyer.

The Ranch was assumed ready for cattle the spring of 1904, and 300 head were shipped in early in April. It is not known whether April was considered a safe date to start pasturing or if the cattle were expected to eat the dead, wild grass standing in the meadows from the years before. In any event no provision had been made to feed the cattle and many literally starved to death. Mr. Nevis told one of the neighboring farmers that the bawling of "…those poor, hungry beasts is driving me crazy." He tried to buy hay locally, but there was little to be had.

The high lands that had been cleared and seeded provided excellent pasture during season, but the main dependence had been placed in the "lush, native meadows." Of course, cattle will not willingly eat bog grasses. The result was that the ranch was overstocked for the existing usable pasture and they broke through fences repeatedly over-running the small farms that were being established at about the same time. Hard feelings resulted. An occasional beef was collected for payment of damages.

Elner Strom tells of the ranch cattle ranging across the McGregor bog as far north as the Northern Pacific railroad.[87] They would get on the railroad grade, especially at night, to get away from the mosquitoes and flies. Quite often a train would kill one or several head.

Minnesota at one time had a free range law such as exists today in some western states. Cattle were free to roam at will. Few of the settlers had their lands fenced and cattle might graze over several miles, trying to find a little grass among the stumps and brush. Quite often the small herds of several settlers would range together.

Once during the summer of 1904, a herd of native cattle met a bunch from Davidson McRae's herd on the Northern Pacific grade near Blueberry Siding. They fought, as strange animals often do. A train came along during the fight killing over thirty head of cattle. The settlers were quite irate that the ranch herd was loose. Just why their cattle should be more privileged than the ranch cattle is not clearly understood. In any event the Aitkin County Commissioners adopted a herd law shortly after this. Cattle were required to be either under the care of a herder, or confined on the owner's premises.[88]

Davidson McRae Land Company sold about 1,000 acres to Lando F. Gran of St. Paul, on January 2, 1918. The sale included the ranch headquarters, the fields, and improved upland pasture acreage.[89] The balance, mostly bog and wild meadow, was permitted to revert to the County for non-payment of taxes.

Gran attempted to operate it as a general livestock and dairy farm under the mangership of Charlie Reisinger, hiring a few local, young men to do the farm work. He lost his holdings by a mortgage foreclosure in 1930.[90] Much of this land is now a part of the Rice

---

[87] Elner Strom, personal interview, McGregor, Minnesota, October 1965
[88] Ibid.
[89] Register of Deeds, Aitkin County, Davidson McRae Stock Farm Company by deed to Lando F. Gran, recorded in Book 20 of Deed Records, p. 522, Jan. 2, 1918.
[90] Register of Deeds, Aitkin County, Mortgage foreclosure recorded in Book 46 of Deeds, p. 169, Oct. 6, 1930; Book 46 of Deeds, p. 288, Feb. 6, 1931; Book 46 of Deeds, p. 389, May 18, 1931.

Lake National Wildlife Refuge, U. S. Department of the Interior at McGregor, Minnesota.[87]

There was one interesting chapter in the Ranch's history under Mr. Gran's ownership. Montana suffered a severe, prolonged drought in the early 1920s. In the summer of 1923 Gran arranged to have several carloads of Montana range cattle shipped to his ranch for grazing. They arrived by Northern Pacific railway, complete with authentic Montana cowboys on cowponies, to handle them.

However, the same kind of miscalculation as to the grazing capacity of the land was made as had plagued Davidson McRae in earlier years. In addition to the problems of over-stocking there was the problem of poor fences. Davidson McRae had erected good fences originally, but twenty years later they were in no condition to contain several hundred head of half-starved, half-wild range cattle. They over-ran the countryside, eating up farmers' hay stacks, breaking into farmer's pastures, mingling with native cattle, sometime following the farm cattle into a barn. The cowboys did their best to contain the herd, but it was a hopeless situation. When, finally, the cattle were shipped to South St. Paul for slaughter in the late fall their numbers had been thinned by an angry revenge-bent community.[88]

Barns previously located on Rice Lake National Wildlife Refuge

YERKALA BARN
Photo submitted by Alan Thornbloom

MILLER BARN

KANGAS BARN
Photo submitted by Alan Thornbloom

---

[87] "Personal correspondence of the author, letter from Manager, Rice Lake National Wildlife Refuge, McGregor, Minnesota, June 14, 1966
[88] Family diaries of the author

JOSEPH and HAZEL (ROBINSON) HERUBIN

In 1924, Joseph Herubin purchased 40 acres in Section 8 of South Millward Twp. They moved to the acreage in 1925 from Carlton County. The original structure on the east side was a cattle barn only, built between 1925 and 1930 of white pine lumber. The picture shows the west side of the barn which was added about 1945. The land had increased to 80 acres. The west section of the barn was used for hay storage. The barn was added onto a couple more times. The whole barn was built with rough sawed lumber. It had a manure carrier inside and 20 cows were milked daily with 5 cans of milk being picked up each day and taken to the McGrath Creamery. The cows were milked by hand until 1965 when the first milking machine was purchased.

The barn was razed in 1984. Joe was also known as an avid trapper during these years. The picture was taken after 1956, as you can tell by the car.

Son Jon and his wife Joanne (Mickelson) now live on the land.

Story and photo submitted by John Herubin and Esther (Herubin) Kubat

HAGMAN BARN

The barn was built by Arnold Eld around 1943. The farm was originally homestead land. He cut all the trees on the farm. He rented a saw mill and did not have a tractor; so he put the belt around the rear tire on a Model "A". The lumber was rough and sawed by Arnold, a very slow process, with the belt being thrown off often!! Willard and Lois Hagman bought the farm in 1947. They added a few additions to the barn.

Story and photo submitted by Debbie Janzen

ANDREW and AILI LAKE BARN
SPENCER TOWNSHIP

The barn was built in 1949 by Henry Boudreau and Gene Insley at a cost of $10,000.00. Andrew and Aili Lake had just moved to the property when it was built the summer of 1949. This barn replaced a smaller barn on the farm.

The barn was a Wisconsin Style barn with a bull pen, maternity pen, and a calf pen. A milk house room was built in the corner. The barn was 70 feet long x 34 feet wide and the height was 48 feet to the top of the cupola.

The barn survived the 1950 flood. During the flood, a boat was used down the center aisle. The livestock were moved during the flood.

The barn burned down a week after Easter in 1970.

Side note Andrew Lake got gored by a bull in 1946. His dog distracted the bull and was killed. A neighbor then put the bull down. This barn with a bull pen never had a bull. The cows were bred by artificial insemination.

Story and photos submitted by Robert Lake

SWANSON BARN

The Swanson barn located in Nordland Township was built at the turn of the century by Erick Swanson. Erick was the postmaster of Glory and ran the grocery store as well. He preached on Sundays at the chapel out back behind the house and barn.

Story and photo submitted by Randy Wall

MAGNUS and INGA HAGMAN BARN

In 1881, Magnus and Inga Hagman took over a homestead of 160 acres. The farm was located in Kimberly Township by the Kimberly Bridge in Kimberly.

Story and photo submitted by Debbie Janzen

MARTIN OPPEGARD BARN

The Oppegard barn was built in 1911. Martin Oppegard had someone build the barn for his family and family business. The barn was located in Kimberly Township.

Story and photo submitted by Randy Wall

LEE BARN

Olof M. and Anna Lee emigrated in about 1888 from Norway to Superior, Wisconsin. In 1892, they moved to Lee Township (named after the Lees) to a log home and barn

A new house and barn in the picture were built in 1900. Both structures burned in 1944.

Story and photo submitted by Doris Nordean

JAMES and ELLEN HANLON BARN
AITKIN TOWNSHIP

I remember the farm when I was very small. It was owned by people by the name of Heglunds. They had it as a dairy and sold milk to customers around town. One of the buildings near the house was called the dairy house.

James and Ellen Hanlon moved on the farm I am most sure in 1938. They also continued as a dairy.

The barn I'm sure was at least 70 feet long (*per Terry Hanlon exact measurement was 90 feet long*). They discontinued milk cows and had started raising beef.

It was in the early 1970s when the barn was hit by lightening and burned. The Hanlons were visiting their boys in the Cities at the time of the fire and neighbor Art Jensen had to call them with the tragic news. The Hanlons built a low metal barn to replace the old barn.

Story and middle photo submitted by Pearl Jensen
Photos submitted by Terry Hanlon

HISTORY of FIELDER and SONS DAIRY

The silo that is featured in the picture of the barn taken soon after the original construction and at the time the dairy operation start up was set up there as a temporary unit; it was replaced several years later with a cast-in-place concrete silo.

The cast-in-placed concrete silo was constructed by a local contractor who specialized in the slip-form style of silo construction business.

Before the house and barn were constructed on that property, Dad knew he had to obtain and install electrical power in order to operate the planned facility once the structures were completed and in operation.

At that time there was not any rural power available (in fact the REA did not exist yet in that area) so he cut a deal with the Aitkin Power and Light Company which was owned by the Town of Aitkin and operated a diesel generating station west of Aitkin National Guard Armory that supplied the electrical power to the town of Aitkin.

He paid for construction of an overheard power line from the last most western Aitkin municipal power drop to the farm site to secure the required electrical power.

FIELDER'S SALES BARN

In 1948 the state of Minnesota passed a mandatory Milk Pasteurizing Law on bottled milk. At that time my folks shut down their Dairy Bottling Operation. They then sold their milk to the Aitkin Creamery.

In 1954, my folks sold the dairy herd and started the Fielder's Sale Barn. Sales were on Tuesdays. Once a month they had a Machinery Auction along with miscellaneous items. My folks did their own clerking and my dad was the Auctioneer. There was a lunch counter inside the building and my mother would prepare food and bake many different kinds of goodies. Her pies and homemade donuts were always the biggest hit. The Sales Barn was very successful and it also became a weekly social gathering.

About 1965 the National Farmer Organization strikes and the prices of cattle took a dramatic toll on Auction Barns. The whole economy was bad. In November of 1967, my folks were forced to close the Sales Barn.

I hear wonderful stories all the time about the Fielder's Sale Barn. Even 46 years after closing. "WOW"....

Stories and photos submitted by Thomas L. Fielder
(youngest child of Francis and Eleanor Fielder)

CARL L. and CLARA (MIDTHUN) WICK

The farm bordered Cedar Lake, four miles west of Aitkin, just past Cedar Brook and the former Cedar Brook Resort south of Highway 210.

They purchased the farm in 1949 from Bert Dibble and took occupancy in June 1950, farming the land and milking Guernsey cows until 1967 when they sold to Scharrer's.

The house is still standing and occupied but the barn is gone, and a house replaced it. The fields were also platted into lots and a number of houses built.

Incidentally there used to be a "town site" just west of the Wick farm called CEDAR LAKE and when we moved to the farm in 1950, there was still a working store on that site, owned and serviced by a Mr. Hamdorf. It was totally stocked with general merchandise and Mr. Hamdorf ran the store. (I believe that it had been a switching site for the railroad at one time, hence the need for the store.) Maybe the passenger train that ran between Duluth and Fargo stopped there.

Story and photo submitted by Joan (Wick) Thompson

JENS OLSEN BARN

This barn was one of the oldest barns in Fleming Township. Jens Olsen owned it until 1976 when it was bought by John and Katy Johnson. It was torn down in June 1988.

A house on the property was built in 1911 and was ordered from the Sears and Roebuck catalog. The house was moved in 1990 to Joe and Ruth Courier's farm.

Story and photo submitted by Katy Johnson and Sara McCormick

HANS and LAVERNA BUHLMANN
Buy a Farm ~ Their Story
Story and photos submitted by Diane Gehlers and Ruth Hauge

Hans and Laverna Buhlmann purchased the farm then on Route 1, Farm Island Township. The buildings including the house were in bad shape, clearly needing several coats of paint. Ruth was 3 years old at the time and described the house as "dirty". The year was 1937.

The renters who had lived there for two years had come from North Dakota because of the drought. They fed their cattle swamp grass which did not have much food value. Many died and were left in the barnyard and some even in the barn. The renters had also piled manure in a large room near the cow stanchions. Hans, known to us kids as Papa, had to drag the bloated dead cattle to a swampy pothole out in the field to deteriorate. He then dug out the manure and hauled it out to the field with only the aid of a team of horses.

The Federal Land Bank that had owned the farm provided a well as part of the purchase which then increased the price of the 120 acres to $1,900. The cattle were purchased from my grandparents, John and Bertha Emch.

Hans and Laverna worked very hard to improve the farm. A cistern was put in near the well and a windmill was built by Uncle Hank Emch, a carpenter by trade. Papa dug a pipe line to a water tank next to the barn for the cattle. A six foot trench was also dug by Papa to the house to provide cold running water in the house. All this had to be done by hand. The barn was obviously very rickety and plans were made to build a new barn. Papa logged out of our woods many logs that provided many feet of lumber. Note the sawdust pile in one picture that came from having the logs cut into boards. Uncle Hank was again in charge of the building crew. The concrete was poured for the basement, cement blocks were laid, and a cap or floor of the haymow was in place. What a sight to see the rounded rafters in place, held there with just a few boards to keep them standing in place. It was late afternoon in September 1947 the tornado hit!

The old barn collapsed and the new barn rafters fell like dominos. Luckily the cows were not yet in the barn for evening milking. They had to be led into the horse barn to be milked and they did not respond well to their new surroundings.

But Uncle Hank prevailed and soon had the new barn up and running before winter. What a beautiful red barn it was. The present owners had it torn down and sold the house which was moved to the "short cut" road now in Aitkin. The only building left on the farm is the granary which had also been built by Uncle Hank.

At the Aitkin High School second all class reunion, Ruth, Janie, and Diane drove out to look at the old farm only to discover that it did not look at all the same. The old granary was surrounded by huge shiny pole barns. All the trees were gone, the orchard was gone, the house was gone, and the beloved beautiful red barn was **GONE** too. We stood with our arms wrapped in a group hug and cried!!

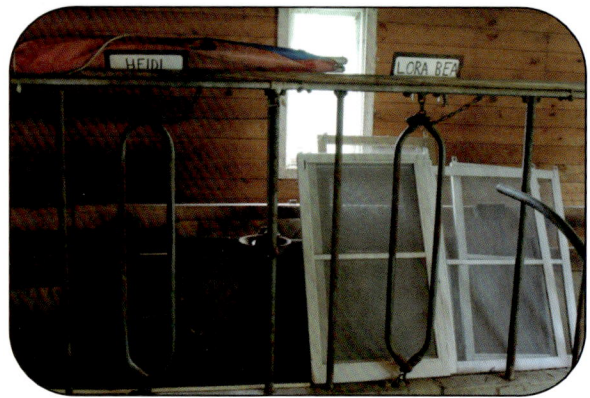

HELLEKSON BARN

The barn was built in the mid 1930s and was purchased by Beatrice (Sprague) and Spencer Howard Hellekson, Sr. in 1939. It is located in Farm Island Township on Thornton Lake. The barn was torn down in early 2000s. A "sister barn" was built in 1952 that still stands across the driveway and is now sided with aluminum. Names of cows still hang over stalls. Each grandchild had a cow named after them. Grandchildren came each summer from their homes in Minneapolis and other cities/states. The land is still owned by Bea and Spence's grandchildren: Sue (Hellekson) Daniello and her husband Dennis (3rd generation), Heidi Blake Anderson (4th generation), and Lora Beatrice Anderson (5th generation).

Story and photos submitted by Sue (Hellekson) Daniello

FRANCIS JOHNSON BARN – 1951
Photos submitted by Marge Johnson

THE JONES FARM

Herbert W. Jones, a physician and surgeon at both Asbury and Northwestern Hospitals in Minneapolis, had a large farm located south and east of Red Top. It was in Sections 25, 26, 27, 33, and 35 of Idun Twp., comprising a total of 2,120 acres and could be reached from State Hwy 65, or from a road going south from the Soo Line 203 crossing. Section 26 included only the SE ¼ and Section 33 included only the NW ¼ of the NW ¼. The old Soo Line Railroad crossing has been known as Jones Crossing for decades, and what remains of the road that went south is still know as the Jones Road. The road was built in 1915 when Gustave R. Zickrick, a land developer in Wahkon, donated $100 to Idun Twp to build a road from Red Top to the Hay Creek Settlement. Hay Creek was to build the part of it in Kanabec County. The road went all the way through to what is now State Hwy 27. The road to the Jones' Farm went east from the north-south road.

One could presume the farm was built in the late 'teens to around 1920. There were two large barns and a nice house with a fireplace. For its day, the farm was quite modern. The house and barns had running water, even though there was no electricity.

Dr. Herbert Jones Farm - Idun Twp, near Red Top, MN   Late 'Thirties

On a hill, centrally located among the buildings was a huge concrete and tile cistern tank. A windmill powered water pump stood over the top of the cistern. An underground water pipe fed water to the buildings via gravity. Doc Jones spent a lot of time off and on in the area, and sometimes performed surgery at the old Isle Hospital. He was even known to have given a "cut-rate", so to speak, on surgery for people in financial straits.

Doc came up to his farm just about every weekend, in his big Pierce Arrow automobile, driven by his driver/mechanic. Quite often, Doc Jones would pick up transients or skid-row types from Washington Avenue in Minneapolis and bring them up to the farm to do work for board and room. They usually worked for a few weeks, sobered up, then left for a return to their old ways. Occasionally, some of them stayed sober. Doc Jones also had a farm in Cottage Grove, Minnesota.

Once, Doc Jones bought sheep and had them shipped into Red Top on a double tiered box car. Unfortunately, many of the sheep died in the freight car from the heat. Another group of the sheep died on the five mile drive from the Red Top Stockyard to the Jones' Farm.

The farm was made up of many sections and parts of sections. Doc Jones had this land surveyed in 1926, and had it fenced in. To this day, you can still find barb-wire grown into trees where the fence lines were.

The timeline is a bit murky in the early days. The property was quit-claimed to Doc Jones and his wife Margaret in 1936 by one Roderick D. Peek (1902-1974) of Hennepin County. Doc Jones was well known in the Red Top area early on. He bought the original Red Top Store building and had it refurbished after the only other store burned down. Peck's mother's maiden name was Daniel or Daniels as was the maiden name of Margaret Jones, who Dr. Jones married in 1909. One of Dr. & Mrs. Jones sons was also named Roderick. The other two sons were Herbert Jr. and David. It seems probable the Roderick Peck was a nephew of Mrs. Jones.

After Doc Jones died at age 66 on July 9, 1940, his family abandoned the farm and it went back for taxes. The east barn was torn down for the lumber during World War II. The rest of the building just sat until 1968, when Aitkin County tore them down. They then planted pine and spruce trees in the fields and grounds.

All that remains today is the stone and concrete foundations, the caved in cistern tank, one of the barn roof ventilators, and some junk piles.

Allan Cummings Barn

Steve Carlson Barn

Photos courtesy of Aitkin Independent Age and Aitkin County Historical Society

* Note - Some of these barns are still standing.

Davis Livery

1918 Gleason Barn

Proesch Barn

1916 Kirsch Barn
Alvin Pearthree threshing

Newstrom & Hartman Livery

FLESLAND - JONES BARN

My Dad's Aunt, Olaf and Blanche Flesland, purchased the farm in the early 1950s. Before that I think it belonged to Pete and Tekla Peterson. The small lake on the property is named Little Pete Lake for him. The barn had to be well over 100 years old. My Uncle Ole used to sit way up in the barn on a platform and shoot deer out the slit in the peak of the barn. He milked several cows and was still doing so when I started coming up to the farm from Illinois in the early 60s. There were other outbuildings, but they have been long since taken down. My parents, Bill and Lucille Jones, purchased the farm from Aunt Blanche just before her death in 1970. They retired up here in the early 80s. My dad was a retired Methodist pastor and before his stroke in 1996 had come out of retirement and was at Cascade United Methodist Church in Deerwood. At some point he had Wes Vall do some renovation to the barn and installed a new roof, which was in perfect shape until it was burned to the ground in 2013. The logs were crumbling, but other parts were still in good shape. My parents sold the farm in 1997. The farm is located on Cedar Lake access road. Many people remember seeing the barn on their way to the lake.

Story and photos submitted by Becki Jones

Inside These Proud, Strong Walls

For a century or more this barn has stood
Proud and strong built by hands as proud and strong.
Animals called it home, kept safe from winter's blast.
They were born, fed, slept and died inside these proud, strong walls.

Generations of children have happily played.
In a world of their own, they pretended to be
Pirates and princesses, Indians and pioneers.
They could be anything inside these proud, strong walls.

Farmers earned their way with this barn's help.
It held their lumber, sawed by hand, dry until there were other plans
Unsuspecting deer became winter's fare as the farmer sat unseen
High up inside these proud, strong walls.

This barn served as a landmark for tourists and travelers,
Hauling boats and poles, looking for fun.
They knew they were close
When they saw these proud strong walls.

Years have come and gone as have the farmers
Children no longer play inside these walls.
Only mice and pigeons now call this home.
The walls, once tall and straight, are crumbling and soon to be no more.

But memories of all still linger, the walls remember all they have seen.
The children still remember
Being pirates and princesses, Indians and pioneers
Inside these proud walls.

By Becki Jones, 2013

GEORGE and NETTIE BOYER BARN
Morrison Township, Section 36
Photo submitted by Diana Rian

CONRAD KELLERMAN BARN
Aitkin Township
Photo submitted by Kenneth Kellerman

WOODROW and ELIZABETH BOYER BARN
Morrison Township, Section 25
Photo submitted by Diana Rian

CHARLES and ELIZABETH VIEBAHN BARN
Aitkin Township, Section 23
Photo submitted by Diana Rian

The Barn

I remember how the barn
Was part of my growing years.
Lots of work and some fun
Mixed in with some tears.

I know how I often cried
When I learned a cow or calf had died.
Or my favorite cat's in Heaven now,
It got laid on by a cow.

There were potholes in the old dirt floor
Filled with brown water and much more.
Often camouflaged by straw
Oops! "Another wet foot, Ma!"

Finally we got a floor of cement.
A Blessing, for which it was meant.
We still had the barn to clean.
A barn-cleaner was just a dream.

We played with our little red wagons
On the new cement floor
Or we'd ride the bicycle
Right out the back door.

All summer we'd mow away the hay.
Sometimes we'd hope for a rainy day.
Then the hay went to bales of square.
But the hard work was always there.

Then the barn got 'Old and Gray'
Sadly a storm took it away.
It was hard for me to see it go.
For I had come to love it so

By Pearl Jensen
June 3, 2013

GEORGE and STELLA KREINER BARN

My father, George Kreiner bought the farm during World War I before 1918. From stories told to me, I don't think the owners were farmers – thus I'm convinced my Dad built or had the barn built.

The barn was (I'm sure) 36 feet wide and 70 feet long with a gambrel roof and very high haymow and 10 feet high ceilings in the lower part. He had few barn dances for a short time. He met my Mother and they married in 1924 and started milking cows.

The tornado in 1934 shifted the barn somewhat. My Dad put a long heavy cable from the barn to a nearby tree for support.

My brother, in later years discontinued milk cows and raised beef. Around the year 2000, a very severe storm hit and demolished the barn.

Story and photo submitted by Daughter, Pearl Jensen

The Barn ~ Part II

A while before my time
When the barn was brand new
People would come to dance, a
Polka and a waltz or two.

Soon the barn filled with cows
And they were born to eat!
Grain, and hay from the mow.
Corn silage was a treat.

All of the cows
Each had her own name.
Nora, Dora, Cora, Flora
For these I'm to blame!

Once in awhile a door,
It would slip off the track.
To lift it back on
Was a pain in the back.

I remember the time when
The bull attacked my Dad
A scary experience
For anyone to have.

My how all the memories
Still seem so fond
Of the Barn's "Good Old Days"
That have all come and gone.

By Pearl Jensen
June 28, 2013

Ed Wall feeding sheep. Ed Wall in barn door. Taken at Thor farm in 1940s.

John & Adeline Swing farm.

Barn in Thor.

Wall farm in Thor.

Photos submitted by Randy C. Wall

Matt & Ida (Swanson) Nickander

McGrath Historical Society

Stories and photos submitted by
Carol Bailey and Darlene Maciej

McGRATH LIVERY STABLE

The first livery stable in McGrath was opened in 1909 by Herman Raduenz. After his sister, Martha, married August Hengel, Herman sold the livery stable to August. In 1914, a new stable was built for August Hengel by Jake Evans and his sons, Clarence and Art. The new barn was kiddy-corner from the old barn on Third and Cedar in McGrath. The old livery stable was converted into a chicken coop.

The new livery (pictured) contained in the front third of the barn the office and storage of buggies, carriages, and sleighs. A trap door in the ceiling with a hoist was for additional buggy storage. The back two-thirds of the barn were used for horse stalls with hay and oat bins above.

When the automotive industry grew, Hengel built the Motor Inn which left the livery stable to sit empty for many years. The barn was torn down in the spring of 1995.

HAROLD and FREDA (KELLING) ASP

Peter Asp had immigrated to Willmar, MN from Sweden. His first child, Harold, was born in Willmar and came to Section 25, Seavey Twp with his parents in 1918. They lived in a small cottage for a year until they could build a home.

Harold married Freda Kelling of Jewett Twp in 1942. In that same year, they purchased a milk and cream route and for the next 21 years hauled milk to the Isle Creamery.

In 1943, they purchased the former John Allison farm located in Section 29 of Pliny Twp eventually increasing their land holdings to 280 acres. In the early 1950s, both a new house and a new barn were built by a builder from Braham to update the property. They raised dairy and beef cattle. The farm has always been well kept and clean. They worked hard to make it so.

BURTON and DONNA RAE (CURTIS) ASP

This farm located in Section 29, Pliny Twp at the junction of State Hwy 65 and County Rd 26, has had several different owners.

This property will forever be known as "Fields Corners" to anyone who lives in this area. One of the first McGrath residents in 1901 was John and Gina (Ekern) Fields. They lived in the SW corner of this junction. Hence the name of "Fields Corner" became a permanent location to everyone.

DeVan Danielson, who was married to Mabel Fields, built the barn on this property in 1935. Art and Florence Rose briefly lived here before Burton and Donna Rae Asp purchased the property in 1969. Harold Asp, Burton's father, whose land was to the west used the barn to house his young cattle. They did not have milk cows as Burton worked the mail route from McGrath to St. Cloud every day.

Burton helped his father with work on the two farms. Burton was killed in 2007 in a farming accident.

WALTER and BERNICE BARTELMA

Walter and Bernice Bartelma made their home in Section 17, Pliny Twp just north of Walt's parents on State Hwy 65.

A small barn and house were already on the property. The barn was a smaller structure on this property of 80 acres. They milked only seven or eight cows. The milk was hauled to the McGrath Creamery by Harold Asp. One feature of this smaller barn was a partition through the middle and in that way, the small herd of cattle could be kept warmer. There is a lean-to on the west side of the barn. They quit milking cows in the late 1950s. They raised beef cattle after that.

Bernice still resides on the farm.

JOHN and ANNA BARTELMA
REINHARD and HELEN (ASP) DANIELSON

John, Anna, and son Charles came to this area from South Dakota and settled north of McGrath in Section 20 of Pliny Twp along State Hwy 65 on 160 acres of land in 1911. John arrived by immigrant car with their horses and belongings. Anna and Charles came in a passenger car. It was all woods at that time. They had to clear the land. A two story house was moved onto the property and eventually a barn and silo were built. They milked cows and sent the milk to the McGrath Creamery. Harold Asp was the milk hauler.

After 20 plus years, the farm was sold to Reinhard Danielson. Reinhard and Helen Danielson purchased the property about 1943. They had cows, pigs, and chickens. Reinhard also drove a school bus for the McGrath School District. He built a garage for the school bus on his property. In 1965, they quit milking cows and raised beef cattle after that.

Helen still lives on the farm at age 94.

STANLEY and THELMA (DRIVER) BUCK
ERWIN and DORIS (BASHORE) BUCK

The Stanley Bucks had a farm near Mora, MN in the early 1930s when they decided to move further north to McGrath. They settled in Section 31, White Pine Twp with their three children--Norman, Maureen, and Erwin (age seven). They built a small house with a square silo on the corner of the property. Erwin and his father were in the rescue party to help find James McGrath in 1940.

Erwin received seven purple hearts and a bronze medal while serving in World War II with the Marine Corps, 4th Division. He has received many honors for his service to his country.

Erwin married Doris Bashore in 1948 and they began farming to the south of his parent's homestead. There have been three barns on this place; two were struck by lightning. Only three cows were lost in the first fire. The second time with the help of neighbors, all the cattle were saved.

Erwin worked away from home as a bricklayer in Northfield, MN. His wife and children took care of the farm. About 25 cows were milked; the milk was first hauled to the McGrath Creamery, then to Ogilvie, MN. Elgin Kadlec was the milk hauler for them.

Erwin still lives on his home place and has made over 170 grandfather clocks over the years! However as he reaches 89 years of age, that hobby has been given up.

ROY and NELL WINSOR
LYLE ELYEA

This farm located in Section 9, Lakeside Twp was owned by Roy and Nell Winsor in 1921.

The barn was built in 1929 with the milk house on the west side added at a later date. They raised mostly sheep on this property.

After Roy's death in 1966, the property was sold several times, before Lyle Elyea bought it in the late 1960s. He has Holstein dairy cattle and ships his milk by AMPI to Duluth MN.

A story connected with this property: When the Winsors first came here they settled in Section 10 on what later was known as the Hawkinson place across the road, where the Carl Eklund Family lived. It was mutually decided that the two men would "trade" properties. So the Winsors ended up on the west side on Hwy 47 and Carl Eklunds on the east side of Hwy 47. Since then, the Elyea family has purchased the property in Section 10.

When the Elyeas came to this area from Monticello, MN – all three – parents and two sons – were dairy farmers within two miles of each other in Lakeside Twp.

DENNIS and DELORES (ERICKSON) ELYEA

Located in Sections 14 and 15 of Lakeside Twp, owner Dennis Elyea purchased this farm on a Sheriff's auction in 1970.

The Elyeas have added the west and north sides of the barn; added a milk house on the south side and have re-sided and re-roofed the barn through the years. There is a total of three silos on the farm; one being a Rochester.

They milk about 40 cows, slightly more during the summer months. The milk is picked up by AMPI every other day for bottling in Duluth, MN.

This farm is one of the last seven operating dairy farms in Aitkin County as of 2013.

STANLEY and MAE (MILLER) FLOREK

All that is left of this farm are the house and silo. It is located in Section 35, Malmo Twp, right along Cty Rd 2.

Stanley farmed here for many years. The unique part of the barn was that the cattle shed was almost underground, with the haymow being above ground. By having it built in this way, a person could drive in the south end of the haymow, unload your hay load and back out again. There was an entry/exit door for the cattle at sub-level.

Stanley was killed in a farm accident in the fall of 1957. After farming operations ceased, the framing part of the underground barn began to deteriorate and the wood frame had to be removed. Dirt was hauled and a bulldozer was used to cover the foundation. The silo still stands today.

This property currently has several owners and is listed in the Aitkin Cty plat book as Rocky Ridge Ranch.

RON and JAN GALLION BARN

Alvin and Marion Gallion married in Missouri before coming to this area. Alvin was born in nearby Mille Lacs County.

Their farm of 200 acres is located in Section 26 of Lakeside Twp. They milked cows. Their milk cans were numbered 366 and 367. The milk was hauled to the Isle Creamery by Haven Damar.

They had six children. Their sons, Larry and Ron raised cattle in a couple of the lean-tos.

In 1956, it was decided to build a barn. Miracle Barn Builders, Alvin and his uncles Herbert and Floyd built the cement block foundation. This is probably the only "round roof" barn in this area. Emil Kadlec from McGrath worked with the men to make the roof.

This farm is still in the Gallion name with Ron and Jan Gallion living on the farm.

OSCAR and ELIZABETH HENDRICKSON
ROBERT and RICA (BARNEVELD) KIMBALL

Bob and Rica (Barneveld) Kimball returned to the area they were born in after World War II-previously having lived in Minneapolis. They briefly lived at a placed called the "Parker Place" just north of Malmo, then moved to the Oscar and Elizabeth Hendrickson property in Section 12 of Lakeside Twp in 1946. Oscar had built a very large barn in 1929 on this property. The barn had an attached feed room/milk house. The milk house had a steam room, which was used for cleaning the milk cans for the next day. There was also a cement underground cooler tank for the filled cans prior to being picked up by the milk hauler, Burton Berry. The family also raised about 50 sheep and hogs to be sold in the fall of the year for extra income. The farm acreage was added to with the purchase of the Henry Hill land-bringing it to a total of 440 acres. The Kimballs lived there until 1971 when they were both killed in a car accident and the property has remained unoccupied since then.

HENKEL BARN

On the E ½ of the NE corner of Section 16 in Wagner Twp stands a barn which was built by a family of German Immigrants by the name of Henkel. They came to America in the late 1800s and settled in various locations one of which being Norfolk, Nebraska.

After a few years, they headed to Central Minnesota. Here they settled in an area soon to be known as Giese. They built several buildings for their own farm and several that were the start of the future town. The original barn they built was used as the house until 1986. They eventually built a barn for their livestock. It was in use until destroyed by a tornado.

The next barn to be built is still standing. The family still owns the property.

HOLMEN BARN

Martin Holmen came to this area in 1918. He bought 80 acres of timberland in White Pine Twp, Section 31 near the SE corner, to clear and log off. The barn was built in the early 1930s completely from the logs cut on this property. Martin was helped by his brother-in-law, Fred Kelling. Lumber from the land was also used to build a wooden silo. To have had a wooden silo was almost unheard of. Another feature of the barn was an inside wooden stairway to the haymow (most barns just had a ladder to the upper level). All of the milk cows were on one side of the barn with the young stock on the other side.

Martin married Edna Kelling in 1933. They had met at a local party dance. They had four sons--Ron, Ted, Bob, and Glenn. All the boys helped on the farm. The family raised sheep, turkeys, chickens, and milk cows. The milk was hauled to the McGrath Creamery. When the McGrath Creamery closed, it was taken to Mora, MN. At one point, an addition was put on the east side of the barn. Martin also served on the Creamery Board in this area. He quit milking in 1950.

Martin was one of the first area farmers to farm with machines rather than horses. In 1939, he bought a John Deere tractor. In 1947, Martin purchased a new Cock-Shutt tractor in Mora. It was the first tractor sold from this dealership!

The barn has not been used for many years. Martin died at 91 years of age in 1985

Ted and Bunny (Henkel) Simonson are current owners of this farm.

ROLLIE & AGNES (MILLER) LARSON

This barn, located on Section 4 of Lakeside Twp, was built by Charles Burman in the 1930s.

Rollie and Agnes Larson owned this 195 acre farm for many years. The barn, a fine structure, still stands today. Rollie had a dairy farming operation.

After Rollie retired from the farming business, the farm exchanged owners numerous times. It is currently owned by Eugene and Denise Hanson.

LES ROBINETTE FARM

The Robinette family lived on this farm located in Section 15 of Lakeside Twp until about 1955. The large barn was built by the Robinette family.

HANS and MARTHA (GERHARDSON) JOHNSON

Hans was born within one mile of where he lived his entire life – Section 5, Idun Twp on 280 acres. He was the son of community pioneers, Carl and Bertha Johnson, who had settled in Section 6. He married Martha Gerhardson in 1927.

The barn, which was built in the late 1920s by Hans and his father, Carl was a large structure and housed many animals. The couple had no children, but boarded the Cedar Lake school teacher for many years. They had no electricity or running water in the house.

Because of low ground, a well was never dug. Hans along with his nephew, Robert Zimpel, who lived with his grandparents most of his young life, would haul water from Cedar Lake to the farm to water the animals. Robert helped his Uncle Hans with the farming operations in his young years. With no electricity, the cows had to be milked by hand. The milk cans were picked up and hauled to the Isle Creamery. A silo was built in the 1940s which still stands today.

Martha's nephew, Roger Gerhardson purchased the farm in 1975 after Han's death. He and his wife Joan did not farm the land.

Over the years, the barn deteriorated and eventually collapsed.

LeCOCQ BARN

James and Jenny LeCocq came to the McGrath area from Pella, IA. They had been farming bottom land and were looking for better land. In the early 1920s, they settled in the SE corner of Section 29 of Pliny Twp on 80 acres along the present State Hwy 65. The Snake River runs through the western part of this land.

When they arrived, this area was all woods and so the first task was to cut the trees and clear the land. They built a log house and small barn. Their milk was hauled to the McGrath Creamery until it closed and then it was hauled to Mora, MN. Harold Asp and Darrel Kadlec were the milk haulers.

Their son Paul and his wife, Winnifred Anderson, purchased the farm. Paul added to the barn several times over the years enlarging the inside barn space. They milked 38 cows and their milk can number was 11.

Their family consisted of six children who all helped with the farming operation. The family raised chickens and sold a lot of eggs to tourists coming up to the lake on weekends.

They sold the property in 1999 to Chris Moser.

JOHNSON BARN

This property in Section 6, Idun Twp has only had four landowners. Karl and Britha Johnson were immigrants from near Bergen, Norway who chose this 160 acre farm in 1895. This large barn was built by Karl and his sons. The Johnsons raised horses, cows, sheep, hogs, chickens, and bees.

Alfred and Donna (Green) Johnson (no relation) bought the property in 1970. They had 40 head of Angus cattle and 30 head of sheep. They raised the barn and put a cement block foundation underneath the structure when they lived there.

In 1978, Richard and Virginia Schultz purchased the property. They raised horses and cows for approximately eight years. They had built a milk house on the east side of the barn.

The large barn stood until a tornado took it down in the early 1980s.

AUGUST and LILLIAN MARPE

The year was 1935 when the Marpes were tired of city living. They had come north several times for white fishing and liked the area. They purchased 120 acres in Section 14 of Lakeside Twp.

As they increased their milk herd, both Marpes did the milking chores from 12 to 16 cows twice a day. Their milk can number was 116. Haven Damar hauled their milk to the Isle Creamery.

In 1944, it was decided to build a barn. Two neighbors, Gottfred Long and Elmer Newmann, helped August build the barn. Elmer had built a form for cement blocks and bolted the rows together, thus making a nine level sturdy silo to go with the barn.

The farm was operated until 1962 when it was sold. The farm buildings still stand today as part of a horse ranch.

GREGORY H. and FAYE ZIMPEL, SR.

Harris Zimpel moved with his parents in 1915 to McGrath and settled in Section 21 of Pliny Twp.

A large barn was built in 1938 by Frederick (grandfather) and Harris (son). During the farming years, they had dairy and beef cattle as well as feeder pigs.

Harris took over the farm in 1945 and his son, Gregory took over the farm in 1981. The dairy business ended in 1970. Now only beef cattle are on the land which covers 324 acres in Pliny Twp along Cty Rd 26 and State Hwy 65.

Can you Move a Barn?

The answer is certainly you can!

Maurice Berry, a local man, had a reputation of being able to "move anything". He moved houses, farm outbuildings, and even a church – before undertaking this project.

In the late 1940s, Otto (1869-1954) and Dina (1873-1966) Johnson had a farm in Section 6 of Seavey Twp. Their son Jack had taken over the farming task and wanted to build a new barn on the land. Word circulated around the neighborhood that the old barn would be for sale. Morton Bertels who lived in Section 12 of Lakeside Twp was in need of a barn and so the deal was made.

In 1948, in preparation to make the move the upper part of the barn had to be lifted up or jacked up from its fieldstone foundation. (In those days, it was common practice to have the ground floor of a barn made out of fieldstone. By picking up rocks from the land and putting them into a "form" and then using a mortar to hold them together a wall was constructed.) This done, a short-wheeled road tractor was driven into the center of the barn. Two large lumber planks 16" to 8" square were laid lengthwise and went through some steel boxes that Maurice had made, to make it possible for the barn frame to ride on the fifth wheel of the truck. Maurice had a GMC truck on the front end of the barn. It was now ready to be moved.

They began by inching forward 1/8 mile towards Cty Rd 2, which was a dirt road between Malmo and State Hwy 65 (220th ST). Turning left (west) on Cty Rd 2 and going ½ mile to a dirt road going south (280th Ave). They had to make a left turn; the barn was wider than the dirt road. A tree had to be sawed down just to get the barn down the road. As they got to a small hill in the road, Maurice's truck stalled. The truck in the center of the barn had to move forward, pushing Maurice's truck to get over the hill. Maurice's truck began to work again!

The move continued southward for one mile going past the Samson land. Only one tree had to be removed along this road. They now entered a wetland area and attempted to turn right (west on 210th LN). This was a very sharp turn and the inside truck tires did sink into the roadbed. By previous agreement, the moving men had made the decision that if the barn should tip over or sink into the swamp they had with them 10 gallons of gasoline and were prepared to burn the barn.

With much effort both trucks lurched forward and made the turn going westward for one mile (210th LN) to the Bertels's driveway. Because of the size of the barn, and the many trees that grew along the driveway, the men elected to go further west to the Bob Kimball farm another 1/8 of a mile and turn left south on a hayfield to cross to the Bertels's land to the fieldstone foundation that was prepared for the barn. The barn had a new home. Bertels used this barn for quite a few years. Shortly, after his wife Beda (Hoyer) died in 1955, Morton sold the land and moved into Isle. This land is now owned by Ron and Marlys Nelson.

WILLIAM and MILDRED (MUMFORD) OTT

William and Mildred Ott first moved to Section 9 of Lakeside Twp on 120 acres around 1926. William purchased the original first Lakeside School, that had been built in 1906, located in Section 10 and with Nealy Johnson numbered the logs and moved the building to Section 9. Putting a ground foundation underneath the old school building, it was made into a barn. The windows of the schoolhouse were boarded up to make the haymow on the second floor (see picture). The school had been closed in 1912. A new school was being built in Section 4.

In 1948, the highway department made a decision to carve out a new north road to Malmo-number Hwy 56, later Hwy 47 and currently Cty Rd 38. The Ott house, which had no electricity or running water, was torn down along with the school, house, and barn. Because the land on the Ott farm had good gravel, it was needed to make the new road. The Ott family moved to Section 33 of Malmo Twp. This property had previously been owned by Dr. Vernon Munson and Oscar & Elizabeth Hendrickson. The most important feature was that the large farmhouse had electricity and running water! A large barn had been built on this property and eventually 3 silos (which still stand) were erected (see picture – before silos were built).

The Ott family numbered nine children, so the new house and farm were a good size for them. William Ott died in 1952. The property has remained in the Ott name for over 60 years.

E. L. PETERSON BARN

The first resident of Eastside Twp arrived in May 1881 from Sweden coming to an area he picked out on a map.

The land was in Section 34, Lakeside Twp. The Petersons being the first settlers in this area opened their home to anyone coming through the area to settle in the new land.

They built a cabin and a barn for the cattle to begin farming. The barn pictured is likely the second or third barn on this farm. Cows were milked and 160 acres of land was cleared.

The original land is no longer in the Peterson name.

PEYSAR/DeBRETO BARN

In 1934, Walter and Minnie (Johnson) Peysar moved to land in the SW corner of Section 7 of Seavey Twp. There had been several previous owners of this land. The Peysars rented this property for a couple of years. In 1938, they purchased the land from Dora Dietzel.

There was a small house and small barn on the property. The first barn was located just north of the current building.

In 1946, a new barn was built by Henry Larson, a local carpenter. He built quite a few barns, but this was his last one. The Peysars milked 17 cows; 13 stood on the south side and 4 on the north side of the barn with a horse stable in the remaining area. They shipped four cans of milk daily. Their milk can number was 126. The milk was taken to the Isle Creamery. Walter was an agent for Madison Silo Company of Madison, MN. In the early 1950s, a silo was built on the south side of the new barn.

The Peysars two sons, Edward and Roger, grew up on this farm. Walter and Minnie lived here until 1979. After Walter's death in 1979, the land was sold and Minnie moved into the town of Aitkin.

The land is now owned by Paul and Teresa DeBreto. The barn is still in daily use.

Photo submitted by Ed Peysar

REIBESTEIN BARN

The Reibestein relation came from west of Princeton, MN. In 1919, Frank and Minnie Reibestein had the opportunity to purchase new land available in Aitkin County. They purchased almost 500 acres for their two sons. Arne and his new bride, Lena received 230 acres in the SE corner of Section 33 of Lakeside Twp. The remaining 250 acres went to their son Carl across the road in Mille Lacs County.

A small house and barn were built by Arne to begin farming. Arne married Lena Stahl of Erskine, MN in 1927 and began homesteading.

In the summer of 1936, the decision to build a larger barn was made. Fifteen year old nephew, Joe Hounder, remembers sawing and piling lumber most of the spring and summer to began the building project. The dimensions of the barn are not documented and the builders are no longer remembered, just that it was a company of builders who worked on the job (Joe's memory).

In the early 1980s, Arne's granddaughter, Sharon Moenkhaus, purchased the farm from Arne. Over the years, she has enlarged the original farmhouse. In 2005, she and her husband Pat began restoring the barn. It has been completely re-sided with red steel siding and a white steel roof and looks extremely nice. It is still a work in progress.

Sharon has honey bees and chickens on the 120 acres of the farm. She leases some pastureland for cattle.

HANS EKEN, ART NELSON
BRIAN and GINA ROTH

The original owner of this land in Section 32, White Pine Twp along the north side of Cty Rd 2 came from Norway in 1902. Hans Eken and family settled along the Snake River. Many men worked in the logging camps before the land was cleared for farming. The wives and children did the farm chores while the men were away. There are no pictures from the time that this family lived at this location. One of the younger Eken sons, Olaf, moved a house across the road, although he did not farm. He spent his adult life working for the Aitkin County Highway Department.

In the 1940s, Art Nelson owned this property. He built the barn and worked the land for quite a few years. The barn still stands even though there have not been any animals on this place for years.

The current owners are Brian and Gina Roth.

ROSEBERG FARM

Located in Section 9 of Lakeside Twp, this barn has been in the Roseberg name since 1917. The Rosebergs came to America in 1901, settling in Pennsylvania. Elof was advised by his doctor to go west. Elof saw an advertisement for a 40 acre parcel of land in Malmo, MN.

With a lot of hard work, they cleared the land of logs and made it into a farm.

A large barn and house were built. Fritz Roseberg took over the property from his father, Elof, farming for many years. Upon his retirement, his son Robert took over operation of the farm.

Robert has sold his dairy cattle and now has beef cattle.

HARLON and JEAN (WOOD) ROTH

The Roth property located in Section 32 of White Pine Twp has never changed ownership. Harlon was born on this property. It was first owned by his parents, Garth and Clara Roth, who originally had come from Iowa in 1918.

The barn on the property burned to the ground in 1951; the first year Harlon and Jean were married. A cement block barn with three silos was built. At one time, he was milking 52 cows a day and the milk was taken to the McGrath Creamery; later to Duluth, MN. In 1963, Harlon was named Aitkin County's Outstanding Young Farmer.

After clearing his land and his neighbors, Harlon decided to sell all the livestock and go into the gravel business.

Both Harlon and Jean are retired and grandson Brian now runs the construction business.

LEWIS SIMONSON (No picture)

On the NE ¼ of Section 20, Seavey Twp there once was a barn built by a Norwegian immigrant family. The head of the family was Lewis Simonson. He and his wife Lenae came to this area from Atwater, MN where Lewis was born and raised. His wife came by ship from Norway to America. They raised a large family on this farm. Ted Simonson, their grandson, recalls that the barn was built in an unusual style. It was a long building with a door on either of the ends so one could enter with a wagon and travel straight through. It was built into a hillside. The lower portion of the barn housed the cattle and horses. There are only remains of the foundations of some of the farm buildings currently at this location.

THE SAMSON BARN

In about 1901, John Otto (1874-1925) and Ingeborg (1866-1929) Samson emigrated from Sweden to Aitkin County. They settled in Seavey Twp, Section 6. Their farm is located 4 miles east on Cty Rd 2 and 1/3 mile S on what is currently 280th Avenue.

There they built a barn, house, and other outbuildings on 160 acres of land. They had a beautiful dairy farm and sent their milk to the Isle Creamery. John served on the Creamery Board for several years.

They raised a family of six children – Joseph, Leonie, Carl, Theodore, Eleanor, and Daniel. All the children were educated at the Seavey (Halstead) #61 School, which was located on donated Samson land on the eastern border of their acreage. Joe was a mailman and was killed in an auto accident. Carl drowned while working on the Great Lakes. Ted and Dan ran the farm after their parents' deaths until the early 1960s. The place has stood unoccupied since Ted's death. The barn, windmill and house still stand after 50+ years.

AXEL SIMONSON BARN

On the SE ¼ of the SW corner of Section 29, Seavey Twp is a barn which was part of the homestead of the Axel Simonson Family.

Axel and his wife Anna lived on this homestead and raised 12 children. The original barn perished in a fire in 1931.

The fire was accidently started by Axel's five year old son Teddy, who was trying to roll a cigar of tobacco leaves. Some livestock was lost and the building completely destroyed due to this fire.

The family thought their son was also lost until he later was found hiding in the orchard. A new barn was built (pictured) and is still standing.

ROY SOWERS BARN

Located in sections 8 and 9 of Pliny Twp, this 120 acre farm is located on both sides of State Hwy 65.

Two barns, one silo, a house, and several other outside buildings make up this property believed to have been built by Roy Sowers.

The barn is most remembered as the *"dance barn"* in the late 1940s and early 1950s. As the picture shows, there was a west side entrance to the second floor. The stairway and platform have now fallen down. But it was *THE PLACE* to be for a Saturday night dance.

The barn is not a large building and the inside downstairs is finished with tamarack logs.

In 1953, this property was sold to Herbert and Audrey Kohlgraf and became a dairy farm. Having three sons, Herbert was known to say, *"That to milk cows kept the boys out of trouble"*.

The round roofed barn (pictured) to the west of the other barn was used as a repair/storage shed for the farm. The milk was hauled to Mora by Harold Asp.

The Kohlgrafs owned and farmed this land until 1991 when they sold the property to their daughter Sharon and husband Melvin Vogt who still live on 20 acres of the original farm.

THOMSEN/PETERSON BARN

Thor Thomsen was one of the first settlers in Idun Twp and had emigrated from Norway with his family at age 18. He lived and worked in several areas of the United States before returning to Minnesota. In 1932, he married Margaret Walters. Her family had settled in Idun Twp in 1915. The new couple lived in Section 11 on 80 acres of land for 10 years. Four children were born into this family.

In 1938 or 1939, Thor built the barn on this place. He was helped in the building process by John Henry Walters, his brother-in-law.

They milked 14 cows and sent the milk to the Isle Creamery. In 1942, they lost ten cows to bangs disease and decided to sell the remaining four. In August of that year, they moved to Seattle, WA to live and retire. When they left this area, they rented their farm to Carl and Rachel Peterson who lived in Ogilvie, MN.

After four years this farm was purchased by them. The farm has been increased to 120 acres. The Petersons had previously lived in South Dakota; moving to Minnesota during the drought years.

Their son Brent, his wife, and family along with Rachel still live on the property. Brent has some cattle, puts up the hay and does cattle butchering for hire. Rachel turned 100 years old in 2012.

THE STEEVES BARN

The Steeves place is located in Section 33, Malmo Twp on State Hwy 47. This family had moved to Malmo in 1922 from Wayanette, MN.

It was just a small farm, but a barn was built. They raised Brown Swiss cattle. After the animals were gone, this place had several other owners.

For many years, a gold star hung in the window of the house in memory of son, James, who died in a Japanese Prison Camp in World War II.

In 2001, Bob Monette purchased this place and has done a lot of work on the house and the barn.

WALTERS BARN

John Henry Walters emigrated from Germany living in North Dakota and Wisconsin. John married Elizabeth Marie Zimmerman in Marionette, WI. They moved west and settled in Section 10, Idun Twp on 160 acres just west of the town of McGrath.

The land in Idun Twp had a lot of trees. They had to clear the land and log it off before making it into farm land.

The building of the first barn and its measurements are not known. The barn was built by John Henry and his two sons, George and Joe. The foundation and lower floor were made from fieldstone rocks, picked from the land, and piled to make the walls.

In 1928, George married Sophie Marianne Thorson. They lived on the homestead and had a dairy farm. They sent milk to the McGrath Creamery and later to the Isle Creamery. They had a family of four; Sandra, John, Gerald, and Charles.

In 1941, the first barn was destroyed by fire. It burned completely down to the rock walls. Other buildings housed the cattle for many years. In 1958, John who was taking over the farm, decided to rebuild the barn. The east wall, which is shown in the photo still stood. He built the barn around this wall and added a metal roof. Acreage was increased to 200 acres. His milk can number was 248.

John married Ernestine Ganz in 1963. They took over the farm. John quit milking cows in 1974 but the farm continues to have Angus Longhorns and horses.

The farm now boasts five generations of Walters who have occupied this farm in Idun Township.

JOHN and EMMA (FAGERSTROM) PETERSON

John Peterson was living in Cokato, MN when his Uncle Nels convinced him to come north to Seavey Twp in 1915. The Peterson land is located in Section 32, Jewett Twp on 80 acres of land along east Cty Rd 2.

He began clearing the land for a future farm while he worked for James McGrath. John also worked making corduroy roads in Jewett Twp to earn enough money to build and finish a house for his growing family.

The family briefly moved to Minneapolis in 1923 before returning back to the "woods" two years later.

Along with milking cows, John had an interest in honey bees. He kept bees and sold honey for a quite a few years-to the extent that he got the name of "Honey" Peterson.

The current owners, Wesley (deceased) and Gertie Peterson (no relation) have done a good job making the farmstead an attractive setting.

THE SAMUELSON BARN

Since December 14, 1899, Samuelson has been the family name on this land in Section 27 of Lakeside Twp in an area known as Eastwood Community.

This hip roofed barn was built around 1910 and was designed to be used for dairy cattle with a large hay loft above. Milk from the farm was sent to the Isle Creamery, until the dairy operation ended in 1979. At that time, a herd of beef cattle was started and the barn has been used each year for shelter during the late winter and early spring calving season.

Third generation, Blanche (Wilbur's wife), fourth generation, David and his wife Elena, and fifth generation Aaron and Michael along with their wives are currently operating the family farm. The daughters of Aaron and Cara and the daughter of Michael and Samantha, are the start of the sixth generation of the Samuelsons to live on this land.

MELSBY BARN

The Melsby name was the first immigrant from near Bergen, Norway to settle on 80 acres in Idun Twp, Section 6. Hans Melsby (Albert's Father) had come to this area in 1892. His brother, Ingvald had built a new cabin on Cedar Lake and let the Idun School District use this cabin for its first schoolhouse. The Melsbys being the first settlers were always helpful to the new settlers arriving each new season.

This land location was on the dividing line of Idun Twp and Mille Lacs County. It was across the road from the future Holden Lutheran Church which was begun in 1895.

The Melsbys farmed these 80 acres, built a barn and house on the land and were residents of the community for many years.

In 1963, the land parcel was sold to Clayton and Judy (Gallion) Peterson for three years. In 1966, Paul and Betty Hemmings purchased the property.

There have been no animals on this place or in the barn since 1993. Eventually, Paul formed a partnership with Tom Hawkins and a sawmill business was started in 1993.

This is a very busy place with truckloads of logs arriving daily for processing into finished lumber to be picked up for delivery by big trucks. This business employs about 12 local workers and is a successful business and benefit to Aitkin County.